The Birdwatcher's Year

Richard
Williamson

summersdale

THE BIRDWATCHER'S YEAR

Copyright © Richard Williamson, 2013

Illustrations by Debbie Powell

All rights reserved.

Summersdale Publishers Ltd
46 West Street
Chichester
West Sussex
PO19 1RP
UK

www.summersdale.com

Printed and bound in Czech Republic

ISBN: 978-1-84953-436-9

Substantial discounts on bulk quantities of Summersdale books are available to corporations, professional associations and other organisations. For details contact Nicky Douglas by telephone: +44 (0) 1243 756902, fax: +44 (0) 1243 786300 or email: nicky@summersdale.com.

A Note from the Author

BEFORE YOU SET off you will need binoculars, preferably with very good light-gathering capabilities to be able to see distant birds properly; aim for lightweights (or they will become tiresome after an hour) with a good magnification factor. To ensure you get a pair with suitable magnification, divide the smaller number into the larger number and avoid anything less than 5, e.g. for 7 x 42 (42 ÷ 7 = 6). Telescopes with much higher (therefore better) magnification will need a tripod to steady them: some prefer them but they tend to be cumbersome.

FOR IDENTIFICATION PURPOSES you will need a pocket guide: my favourite is the *Collins Guide to Birds*, which fits easily into the pocket.

CLOTHING SHOULD BE appropriate to the season: good waterproof boots are often necessary even in summer: take a mobile telephone in case of emergency – food and drink as required! If walking far in an unknown area a detailed map is essential.

THERE ARE CURRENTLY 596 birds on the British list, as seen since 1950 (but many are once-only rarities). Of these, 117 breed here and many are regular winter visitors: of which you will find about 200 species mentioned in the present text.

BIRDWATCHING IS FUN: enjoy!

January

Garden

'WHEN THE DAYS begin to lengthen, then the cold begins to strengthen' is the old saying. Unlike us, garden birds have only 8–9 hours out of the 24 to find food in January. They need regular feeding, so remember Cock Robin is not just for Christmas: he needs you every day in the winter.

WHEN SETTING UP feeding stations, separate them so birds do not waste energy fighting. Flat tables are best for Blackbirds, Robins, Dunnocks (that's Hedge Sparrows) and Collared Doves. To prevent disease, tables should be scrubbed down with water regularly.

NUT FEEDERS AND fat-balls are best for Nuthatches and Tits; Niger seed for Finches, such as Siskins and Goldfinches; loose wheat on the ground for Chaffinches. If buying these is too much for your weekly budget, then household scraps – breadcrumbs rubbed round the frying pan fat, some suet, a handful of currants, even cheese cut up into tiny pieces, bacon rind, melted lard – have saved millions of birds over decades past. Avoid anything too salty.

BIRDS NEED FRESH water every day, preferably in a shallow container. Old frying pans are ideal – they can be easily cleaned and are the correct depth for small, nervous birds, which are frightened of drowning.

MAKE SURE OLD nest boxes are cleaned out if you have not done this already. Be aware that they can be full of bird fleas waiting hungrily for a new host. Wrens often use a single box as a communal dormitory for warmth: 25 have been recorded in one single box, though the first in have to sleep at the bottom of the pile and may be suffocated. However, the combined fug keeps most of them alive on bitterly cold nights. As many as 56 Wrens have been recorded sleeping together in farm straw stacks.

ROBINS ARE ONE of the commonest garden birds, with an average of about 12 million in Britain. Six and a half million Blue Tits also occupy almost every area except mountaintops. But all birds have peak years followed by steep declines. Many go away for the winter as well. Cock Robin might hold the fort in the garden, but his wife may well be taking a holiday down in the south of France for the winter, returning when it gets warmer here.

YOUR GARDEN BIRDS might be pestered by Sparrowhawks. Placing the bird table and feeding stations near a dense prickly bush could save their lives in an emergency.

Woodland

CROSSBILLS ARE THE first nesters in the southern fir forests; they could already be sitting on eggs in January. The cock birds glow bright red and look a bit like small parrots as they swing about high in the conifers. The nests are at the end of branches at any height between 3 and 20 metres. The male may help the female to build the nest, which is of lichen-covered twigs with cup of moss, grass – and even sheep's wool!

THE SMALLEST BIRDS in Britain are the Goldcrest and Firecrest. They live high in the canopy of fir woods, but in January may hunt the forest floor for small insects and can become very confiding. I have had one actually stand on my foot.

RAVENS MAY HAVE been courting as early as December, but are certainly active now. The male is a bit of a show-off with his display – from a good height, he calls with one of his 50 different croaking sounds to make sure the female is attentive and watching, then closes his wings and rolls over onto his back, plummeting to earth like a brick. At the last second he turns right side up and opens his wings again just before hitting the ground. She is amazed, even though she could have seen the same act for the past 40 years.

WOODPECKERS FIND LIFE especially difficult now and many will die. The problem varies: for Green Woodpeckers, the ground might freeze solid sealing off the supply of ant eggs; for Great and Lesser Spotted, they could have a severely depleted supply of beetle larvae in dead timber.

IF YOU OWN or manage woodland, whether mature timber or coppice or shrubs, try to forget that old idea of cutting out dead wood. It plays an important role and removing it can be a death sentence for woodpeckers, Nuthatches and many other species, as it contains the larvae of beetles on which these birds feed.

JANUARY IS THE time to hunt our woodlands for signs of Tawny Owls – the sound of their calls in the dusk or on a moonlit night is exciting. Also look around the bases of old trees for circles of cast fur pellets; these are the remains of mice and voles which the owl cannot digest. By examining these you can find out from the skulls what they have been eating. Bank and short-tailed voles, pygmy, common and water shrews, wood and yellow-necked mice, are the main diet.

Wetland and Coastal

JANUARY IS THE peak time for coastal and inland water birds in Britain. There are 2,296 main sites, holding 1.5 million Geese, Ducks, Grebes, Herons and Crakes of 100 different species, all living in estuaries, harbours, lakes and rivers. There are also over one million waders of 40 different species. Most can be seen from footpaths, seawalls, hides and boats.

THE COMMONEST DUCK at this time of year is the Wigeon, with over 300,000 found here. But you might be really lucky and encounter the rarest, the Lesser Whistling Duck, with just one bird sometimes seen. Others you will certainly see are Mallard and Teal, but you may need your *Collins Guide* to sort out some of the 40 or so other species.

ON AN AVERAGE day you might also see up to a dozen species of wading birds. Waders all leave the mudflats as the tide comes up and they gather into flocks to rest and preen until the tide goes down again, when they can feed once more.

ONE OF THE easiest waders to identify is the Curlew with its 6-inch beak, curving downwards. Even in January on warm days the male will make its liquid bubbling call, which has been described by some as 'links of silver sound'.

NINE HUNDRED DIFFERENT marks on Mute Swan's beaks were used in the Elizabethan Age to claim ownership of the birds. Swans were status symbols and eaten at luxury banquets. Thousands fly into Britain in winter from the east.

WHOOPER SWANS MAINLY winter on Ouse Washes (Cambridgeshire), Martin Mere and Ribble estuary (both Lancashire), and Scottish lochs and firths. Distinguishing marks for these birds include upright necks, yellow rear beak patterns and their call note – *'hoo'* – uttered as a long sigh as breath leaves its body, giving rise to the legend that a swan sings as it dies.

NAMED AFTER THE famous engraver and bird artist, the Bewick's Swan can be seen in winter at Slimbridge (Gloucestershire), Ouse Washes and Hickling Broad (Norfolk), the Arun valley (Sussex) and similar habitats.

WILD GEESE ARE divided into the greys and the blacks: Greylags, Pink-footed, White-fronts, and Bean are greys – Canadas, Barnacles and Brent are black. Roost sites have been the same sometimes for centuries and are all well known: it is easy to find them if you watch the coast for an hour or two.

ALL RSPB AND WWT wetland sites have hides and facilities making identification and watching a social pleasure not to be missed. All have information on the Internet.

Field and Farm

FARMLAND BIRDS HAVE decreased alarmingly over the past 40 years, particularly noticeable in the plight of the once common Sparrow, although farmers are now encouraged to enhance bird-friendly habitats. With a little persistence you will still find the treasures in these areas.

YELLOWHAMMERS WILL FLOCK to dense hedgerows bordering rough meadows. Pheasant feeding strips will hold flocks of Linnets and Chaffinches. Where you see more than half a dozen Chaffinches, check whether some might be their darker and very attractive cousin, the Brambling. Their white rump easily tells the two apart. They breed in Scandinavia, sweep south and west in hard weather, and may even feed in flocks on motorway verges where road salt melts the snow making weed seeds available.

THERE ARE STILL 4,000 pairs of Barn Owls in Britain: Ghost Owl, Moggy and Cherubim are some of the old names for them. They have been known to nest inside rabbit burrows, ruins, tunnels, thatched cottages, dove cotes and church towers, as well as the legendary old barns.

RADAR READOUTS HAVE revealed Lapwing flocks fleeing 70 miles ahead of approaching snow clouds from the north. They may keep going right on down into Spain. Mild winters in the UK will find them on the *Ings* of Yorkshire, washes of Cambridge and the brooks of Sussex.

WATCH FOR THE Woodcock flight out of the woods about 35 minutes after sunset as they leave to feed all night on earthworms in meadows and fresh marshes. They will often take the same route year after year and can be timed almost to the minute. Some 1.8 million winter in Britain, most of these coming in from Eastern Europe and Siberia.

FIELDFARES AND REDWINGS breed mainly in Scandinavia but winter with us and when the berry crops have gone they will feed by daylight on meadows, especially where stock are kept and the worm and beetle population is highest.

ROOKS HANG ABOUT their old rookeries more and more as the days lengthen. Crows keep their territories and give everyone a warning curse if they see a fox (or a birdwatcher) skulking under the trees.

KESTRELS THRIVE ON farmland if there are hedgerow trees and headlands of rough grass. Country folk of times gone by had many names for this useful hunter of mice: Fanner, Fanner hawk, Flutterer, Vanner, Wind-bibber, Windfanner, Windhover. The poem, 'The Windhover', by Gerard Manley Hopkins captures its spirit:

> I caught this morning morning's minion...
>   dapple-dawn-drawn Falcon,
>   in his riding
> Of the rolling level underneath
>   him steady air...

Moor and Mountain

PTARMIGAN MOULT THREE times a year to maintain camouflage. White winter plumage hides them from their worst enemy, the Golden Eagle. It is tough living above 500 metres in Scotland's arctic tundra winter, when the sparse vegetation is covered in deep snow, but the species manages survival in northern climes right across the world from Russia to Alaska.

THE CAIRNGORM CLIMATE in midwinter is harsh for that top predator, the Golden Eagle, too, though Red Grouse are easier to catch than Ptarmigan since they remain speckled brown in winter. Eagle diet also includes mountain hares and red and roe deer carcasses. About 400 pairs of Golden Eagles in Britain are now part of the 1,800 population of these montane birds that includes those in Scandinavia.

MERLIN ARE THE smallest of Britain's birds of prey and were traditionally used only by ladies in hunting. They find it difficult to survive winter on the higher mountains where they breed, so they come down to lower moorlands, and even coastal sand dunes and heathland. They prey on Skylarks and Meadow Pipits.

ONE OF THE most surprising Scottish birds is the Crested Tit, found nowhere else in Britain but common over most of Europe. Even in deep winter this tiny bird, which looks almost like a Blue Tit but with a large crest, stays in the pine woods (living on pine-seed) bordering moor and mountain, especially in the Spey valley.

THE VERY LOWEST moorlands in Britain (more usually called heathlands) can sometimes turn up a real red-letter bird in winter – the Great Grey Shrike, for instance. Just two or three are often found on Norfolk and Surrey heaths. The name 'butcher bird', also applied to the Red-backed Shrike, tells you a bit about its lifestyle. It catches small birds and mammals, lizards and insects, and in time of plenty fixes the bodies on to sharp thorns, to be eaten later during food shortages.

THE DARTFORD WARBLER winters as well as summers on the heathlands of southern Britain. January is actually the cruellest month for this, our rarest Warbler, if the temperature drops very low with heavy snow. There were two seriously bad times for this rather delicate bird, 1947 and 1963. Only ten birds were left after the 1963 month of blizzards, but in ten years they had built back to 350. In Sussex a century ago, this bird was known as the French Blackbird.

Sightings

1
....

2
....

3
....

4
....

5
....

6
....

7
....

8
....

9
....

10
....

11
....

12
....

13
....

14
....

January

15
....

16
....

17
....

18
....

19
....

20
....

21
....

22
....

23
....

24
....

25
....

26
....

27
....

28
....

29
....

30
....

31
....

February

Garden

BY NOW BIRDSONG has already started. Chaffinches have sometimes been recorded in early January in the south but more usually the first week of February. Great Tits too have a usual song-date in the first week of this month. It all depends, of course, on the severity of the weather: but do begin to be aware, and listen out. Song Thrushes started their winter territory claims in November, so on mild days now are in full song and may even have first eggs in February.

BUT THIS MONTH can have a severe backlash with deep snow. Blackbirds will flock to a garden if you turn out the last of all those old windfall apples you saved from the autumn and now spread across the lawn. Many of these birds will be migrants which were on their way back to the Baltic – only to be stopped in their tracks by the weather.

BE SURE TO clear up all accessible spare food after the birds have stopped feeding 40 minutes after sunset, or rats and mice may do this for you.

SOMETIMES WE GET 'Waxwing winters' when these northern forest birds descend into British suburban gardens looking for berries. They can be absurdly tame, so you might easily see that bright red waxy patch on their secondary wing feathers. The earliest recorded mass invasion was 1679–80. A flock of Waxwings calls to one another with a blend of ringing notes that vary in pitch and volume that is attractive and musical. 'Wax Chatterers' is an old name for them; it has been known for Fieldfares to feed adult Waxwings with rowan berries, because the white corners of the Waxwing's mouth give it the appearance of a chick begging for food. In February Waxwings will also feed one another as the pairs bond before breeding.

WINTER WILL MAKE you realise how much your garden birds need shelter. Ivy makes an ideal warm refuge as it raises the surrounding temperature and the shiny leaves act as 'tiles' in keeping off rain. Ivy also gives safety from marauding cats. Bird numbers can double in gardens with dense ivy on its trees and in hedges.

SISKINS AND REDPOLLS are becoming increasingly common visitors to suburban or village gardens near woodland. They are usually in small flocks and enjoy bathing together in very clean, fresh shallow water. Their aerial fluttering is a joy to watch.

Woodland

FLOCKS OF FIELDFARES and Redwings fly into thick woodland for communal roosting. Sometimes they are joined by Starlings, although these tend to prefer dense reed beds or towns and city buildings where there is extra warmth.

SCOTTISH CROSSBILLS ARE a separate race to the English birds – they are larger and have heavier beaks. One of the best places to see them is in the Spey valley woodlands (on the north border of the Cairngorms) where they start nesting this month. Their English cousins may be a bit earlier.

HERONS NOW RETURN to their treetop nest sites and start building or rebuilding their old nests of last year if these have survived winter gales. About 10,000 pairs currently nest in Britain, some on the ground in dense reed beds such as at Marazion Marsh near Penzance and Tring in Hertfordshire. A heronry is a noisy place! These lanky grey birds quarrel over who owns what and steal each other's sticks, screeching and squawking loudly.

HARSH WINTER WEATHER may herald the death of one of our weaker woodland birds, the tiny Treecreeper. Normally they shelter behind loose bark or ivy but Wellingtonia trees introduced over a century ago from California have soft bark with flakey 'tiles' and these can make snug roosts. Old names included Tree-climber, -climmer, and -crawler.

ON FINE, BUOYANT days when weak thermals rise
from open fields, Buzzards will start displaying over
nearby woodland – their mewing calls will attract your
attention. These mini eagles spread their wings wide to
get full gliding advantage to gain height and may even
disappear into clouds before closing them and falling
back to earth in apparent suicidal dives, pulling out at
the last moment. Another necessary bonding display
is for these birds to 'hold hands' (clasp claws) as they
drop to earth at great speed. A sight as thrilling as any
Red Arrows display!

THIS IS THE last full month that our brightest crow, the
Jay, will stay in small groups or pairs before the big
spring gatherings. They will depend now on all those
acorns and hazelnuts they buried in the ground back in
the autumn. Their harsh warning sounds like a sheet of
linen being torn in half.

HAWFINCHES HAVE ONE of the most
powerful beaks of all birds relative to their
size. A crushing force of up to 90 lb is used
to crack open cherry pips (off wild cherry
trees) on which it prefers to feed in winter.

Wetland and Coastal

STILL TIME TO see Purple Sandpipers this month and next when the small flocks of this dusky little wader with its yellow legs and purple sheen gather on the rocky shores of the Scottish and north-east coasts of England and further south below Hunstanton cliffs in Norfolk. Like the Turnstone, it will often allow you within a few yards as it searches for sandhoppers and tiny snails in the seaweed at the edge of the waves. If caught by a wave it swims light as a cork back to the rocks.

MUCH MORE COMMON with over 300,000 birds in late winter is the Dunlin. Over large mudflats such as Ribble, Thames, Mersey, Wash and Morecambe, flocks of thousands fly back and forth at high tide making brilliant white and dark heliogram patterns in endless variation across a hundred metres of sky. These are one of our smallest Sandpipers, brown above, white below. In spring they change into breeding plumage and will have a black patch on their underside.

ABOUT 400 GREAT Northern Divers (often called the Loon) gather mainly around Scottish lochs and coasts this month before returning north to breed. Scapa Flow, the Sound of Gigha and Outer Loch Indaal are the best places but they can also be spotted anywhere in more southern estuaries and waterways, even the Sussex coast. Old names for the Loon (name reflecting its mournful cry) were Greatest Speckled Diver, Gunner, Great Douker, or Imber Goose.

GOOSANDERS PEAK THIS month in the Tay, Forth, Tweed and Windermere. Torpedo-shaped with saw-toothed beaks like an ichthyosaur, they had ancient names such as Harle, Gool Duck, Sawyer, Spear Duck, and Dun Diver.

BRENT GEESE FEEL the stirrings of spring in warm moments and chase rivals in circles even though nesting on the Russian coast is three months ahead, and 2,000 miles distant.

WHITE-FRONTED GEESE (sometimes irreverently called Y-fronts) overwinter on the Severn estuary but more recently in bigger numbers on the Swale, Dungeness and Rye Bay. Though the Netherlands have nearly a million birds, Britain hosts only 1,500, peaking in February.

FOUR HUNDRED EXTRA Bitterns overwinter with us now. They float over the tops of reed beds like a brown heron, though more usually they hide below and you will never know they are there. Another 200 are residents and in another month will reveal their presence when the males 'boom' their mating call.

Field and Farm

THIS CAN BE a hard month for birds on open fields. Heavy snow may cause Pipits, Skylarks, Thrushes and Finches to flee Britain for the continent. Or, if the month lives up to its name of February Filldyke, then floods will move Partridges, Thrushes, Wrens and Dunnocks into less secure places. Kestrels and Tawny and Barn Owls can benefit from flooding of meadows when the vole population has to migrate out of the grass onto the banks.

THE GREY PARTRIDGE is fast becoming a rare bird, unfortunately. As with many ground-nesting birds it is troubled by increased numbers of badgers, foxes and intensive crop management. If you are lucky enough, you may hear the cock birds starting to call *'keev-it'* as pair bonding starts.

MAGPIES OFTEN GATHER into large flocks, especially towards the end of winter. They chase each other through the branches and chatter continuously. Superstitiously thought to be a bird of ill-omen, old names for them were Hagister, Maggie, Meg, Pyet and Pianet.

UP UNTIL THE 1950s many country folk used to net farm buildings at night for the flocks of Sparrows at roost in late winter – a score of birds under a pie crust kept a family going for several suppers. The meat is more protein-rich even than rabbit. But this little bird is under threat also: nowadays there is precious little loose grain lying around for them to feed on.

YOU HAVE THIS month and next to see Hen Harriers in their winter quarters on open farmland and upland. The female is speckled brown with a large white rump patch. The male is mainly ash grey with a white rump and black wing tips. They hunt by day for small birds and mice.

FARMLAND IN FEBRUARY may just give you one of the treasures of the fields – a small flock of Corn Buntings. These used to be for the old cornfields what the Swallow is for the village, or the Cuckoo for the woodlands: a symbol of healthy environment. Today small winter flocks of this chubby brown bunting up to about a hundred strong may still be seen in the downs and wolds across the backbone of England but numbers are falling year by year.

PINK-FOOTED AND GREYLAG Geese can still be seen on the sugar-beet fields and coastal marshes of East Anglia and the arables and lochs of Scotland until the end of the month.

Moor and Mountain

GOLDEN EAGLES NOW return to their eyries. About 420 pairs are found in Scotland and they nest on crags and the tops of large pine trees in really remote places where there is little disturbance. Both sexes are a similar mottled brown in colour but the female is larger (as with many birds of prey).

THERE ARE ALSO about 33 pairs of White-tailed (Sea) Eagles in Scotland with about 12 on the Isle of Mull. You can tell the two species apart by looking at their tail shape as they fly overhead. The Golden Eagle has a longer tail with a black terminal band; the White-tailed Eagle has a short almost diamond-shaped tail, which in the adult is pure white.

MALE PEREGRINE FALCONS, which have been protecting their eyries against other hopeful males, should now be joined by their female partners. Traditionally they nested in remote craggy places far from human disturbance. Now they are protected they have expanded and are frequently found on cathedral spires, power stations and tall office blocks.

PEREGRINES OCCASIONALLY FIGHT each other, especially at the start of the breeding season and have been known to kill a rival. They have very long wings with sharp tips and are capable of dives up to 200 mph, the fastest speed of any bird. They also flap with shallow wing beats and circle. They continually practice aerial interception on other birds as well as with their mates without making contact.

DIPPERS MAY START to breed with first eggs by the end of the month if the winter has been mild. They are found across the west of Britain in mountain valleys with tumbling streams, burns and brooks. They might also breed along slower flowing rivers at waterfalls and weirs. They are the only truly aquatic passerine (perching bird) in Britain. They are deep brown with a white bib and chest and they bob about at the edge of the water or on rocky stones and walk about under the surface hunting for insect larvae such as caddis fly larvae and dragonfly nymphs.

CARRION CROWS LIVE up to their name in the mountains, helping to clear up the bodies of deer, etc. which have died of cold, wet and hunger. Their breeding display starts in February when the male bows to his life partner with wings spread and tail fanned to show how big and strong he is.

Sightings

1
....

2
....

3
....

4
....

5
....

6
....

7
....

8
....

9
....

10
....

11
....

12
....

13
....

14
....

15 ....

16 ....

17 ....

18 ....

19 ....

20 ....

21 ....

22 ....

23 ....

24 ....

25 ....

26 ....

27 ....

28 ....

March

Garden

'March dust on apple leaf brings all kinds of fruit to grief.'

'MARCH MANY WEATHERS' is an old saying, as is 'Comes in like a lion, and goes out like a lamb.' Heavy snow is possible, but it usually melts fast. Another name for March is 'Starvation Month', because in olden times the autumn grain had been used up: berries and weed-seeds too. So it can be difficult for birds which need continued feeding ensuring their bodies are strong enough for breeding. You can carry on with winter foods but by next month peanut feeders should be phased out as peanuts are unsuitable for chicks.

GREAT TITS ARE now in full song and it may surprise you to know that a single bird could have 90 different calls. Birdwatchers jokingly say 'If you can't think what bird it is calling, it will be a Great Tit!'

TIT-NESTING BOXES SHOULD have been in place since last October; it is not too late for Spotted Flycatcher boxes though. These migrants are becoming less common, but they still breed as far north as the Orkneys. Their boxes should be wide and open-fronted and should be placed on a north-facing wall for shade.

DUNNOCKS, ALSO CALLED Hedge Sparrows or Hedge Accentors, are secretive, unobtrusive, sometimes solitary birds creeping about under bushes, but with unusual habits. Not only may a female mate with several males but so will males mate with several females.

ROBINS HAVE BEEN known to nest in old kettles, under cabbage leaves, in flowerpots and even in the bathroom if the window is always open!

COLLARED DOVES SING monotonously now and may drive you mad with their mournful *'Bravo dick, Bravo dick'*, which some interpret as 'I feel sick, I feel sick'.

ONE OF THE most important things you can do for your garden birds is NOT use slug pellets, which kill parents and certainly their chicks. This particularly applies to Song Thrushes, which may already have eggs by now if the weather has been mild. Their numbers are diminishing, so they need all the help they can get. If ever you have the chance to see a nest, do admire the perfect inside shell of hard mixed mud and wood chips, much like the inside of a coconut shell.

IN 2012 THE top ten garden birds reported to the BTO (British Trust for Ornithology) were in order as follows: Blackbird, Blue Tit, Wood Pigeon, Robin, Great Tit, Dunnock, Collared Dove, House Sparrow, Chaffinch and Greenfinch.

Woodland

'As many misties in March, so
many frosties in May.'

IN WINTER IT often seems that there are no birds in
the woods except for Wood Pigeons. In March that
all changes as many start to sing and the woods come
alive. A normal southern woodland of old hazel
coppice with oak standards plus pine and spruce in
planted blocks can easily be home to 45 species of
breeding birds. Pure evergreen woods may have half
that number.

CHIFFCHAFFS ARE ONE of the very first migrants into
Britain. Their normal passage is in the second week
of March and on into April, but in recent years birds
have overwintered here and may sing earlier. Some
birds have been known to sing snatches of their close
cousin the Willow Warbler's song of falling cadence in
addition to their own double note of 'chiff-chaff'.

HERONS, RAVENS AND Long-eared Owls may all have
young this month.

PLANTINGS OF CONIFERS have encouraged the spread of Siskins and Lesser Redpolls. Small flocks of both might whirl around the treetops in March, but more likely they will be breaking up into smaller groups and pairs. Both are tiny, have distinctive forked tails, and mainly will be feeding on birch seeds and catkins. Siskins are yellowish-green, Redpolls are pinkish-brown, the males with carmine foreheads. Check that your Siskin is not the much rarer, similar, Serin.

ALL WOODLAND SHOULD be rich in birds. Search Ordnance Survey maps for footpaths and bridleways that enter old woodlands in your local area and you will be surprised at what they have to offer. A good way to get to know the birds of your area is to map each singing male on a large-scale map of your own making and plot them once a week. You will find that the same bird sings from the same area all the time from March to early June. This will familiarise you with the songs and calls of the various species, and their own particular woodland niche.

THE SMALLEST OF the seven British breeding Tits is the Cole (Coal) Tit. This bird with its white nape stripe will be looking for its nesting habitat in woodland which has large old pine trees scattered about. The song is a high-pitched *'See you, see you, see you'* – but you might not see it, because it could be high up in the canopy of green needles.

Wetland and Coastal

IT IS ALL change in the wetlands. Over one million waders on coastal and inland sites are halved by the third week of March. The numbers of Swans, Geese, Ducks, Divers, Herons and Rails, collectively known as 'wildfowl', drop from over a million to three quarters of a million, likely to be the lowest number since September. Nearly all of them are starting the long trek back to the arctic and subarctic to breed. Some will not arrive on their breeding grounds until May.

BITTERNS START BOOMING this month (though an exceptionally early date of 19 January has been recorded in Norfolk). There are about 30 boomers nationally, of which ten are on the Norfolk Broads, the traditional home of this rarity.

A MIGRANT YOU may never actually see is the Water Rail. Many migrate here in autumn although they go back to their breeding grounds in the spring. These birds creep quietly along, hiding in the bank herbage of inland streams. They are the size of a Blackbird with a chocolate brown back and grey undersides stippled to resemble shivers on the pond surfaces and the smallest ripples in streams.

March

JACK SNIPE ARE even smaller and more secretive. They seem very reluctant to fly, because hunting dogs have been known to pick them up out of the rushy couch where they are hiding. Their plumage is a beautiful contrast of deep cream stripes and dark bottle green. Snipe proper are 2 inches bigger. The male sings by calling *'tick-tick-tick'* and seeming to bleat like a lamb by allowing air to vibrate its outer tail feathers ('drumming') as the bird dives. This can be heard up to half a mile away.

ROLE REVERSAL IN the Red-necked Phalarope intrigues bird watchers. Only the occasional bird will ever be seen in Britain but storms can blow them inland off the oceans onto ponds. Their needle beaks and bouncy, floating behaviour immediately attracts attention. In their arctic breeding grounds the female courts the male with her brighter plumage and lays the eggs – but he hatches them out and then looks after the young by himself until they fly.

ONLY 100,000 KNOT remain this month (down from three times that number in midwinter) on the mudflats of the Wash, Ribble, Solway and similar open spaces. Even so there is still time to see their spectacular aerial dance as they swirl about in the seascape as Starlings do in the townscape.

Field and Farm

MARCH IS A very variable month: dry and/or stormy. Increasing daylight makes the birds think of breeding. Flocks of Pee-wits (Lapwings) vanish from the fields in the first and second weeks, splitting up into pairs on the hills and downs of the south and pastures of the north and west. Those that stay display by 'tumbling' through the air, then flap with thudding wings, calling with sweet cries of '*pee-e-wit*'.

SKYLARKS SING AT their best from March to July. Their song was captured by composer Ralph Vaughan Williams in his rhapsody for violin *The Lark Ascending*, inspired by George Meredith's poem which begins:

> He rises and begins to round,
> He drops the silver chain of sound...

LITTLE OWLS NOW begin their spring song. As with the Great Tit, *Athene noctua* has a great variety of calls: a loud and startling '*kiew-kiew*' is one; a rapid, quavering twitter which is shrill and loud but in a minor key; or they can coo, or scream like a Peacock. The Latin name refers to the fact that the Ancient Greeks noted that a bird sat on the shoulder of the statue of the goddess of learning, Athene, daughter of Zeus: hence the phrase 'the wise old owl'.

March

FARMS AND VILLAGES are the traditional homes of Swallows, a few of which can arrive on the south coast as early as the first week in March. Even on the east coast first arrival dates can be as early as 8 March. The bulk of them are in early April.

SEARCH THE WOOD Pigeon flocks for the rarer Stock Dove. Very often the Stock Dove keeps separate from its relative and occasional flocks of 400 have been recorded. This much darker dove is also far less destructive, eating mainly the seeds of knotgrass, charlock and fat-hen. Late this month it will return to its breeding sites in hollow trees.

JACKDAWS START FLYING high up and far from their winter roosts as they scan the countryside for suitable old trees in hedgerows or chimney pots in lonely cottages for nest sites. They are then a tempting prey for the Peregrine Falcon, which the Jackdaw seems to forget about in the excitement of spring.

MISTLE THRUSHES OFTEN prefer open farmland with old hedges to woodland, and often favour village and churchyard trees. This month they sway about in the tops singing loud challenges to the gales – earning their name of 'Stormcock'.

Moor and Mountain

MARCH BRINGS THE arrival of the Ring Ouzel to the moors and mountains. The male looks like a Blackbird but for a white band across its chest, while the female is slightly speckled black with a grey band over her breast. There are two dozen names for this bird, which include: Rock Thrush, Ring Thrush, Rock Ouzel, Tor Ouzel and Ring Blackbird. The wild whistling song carries well across the silence and solitude of lonely moorlands. The song is simpler and louder than the Blackbird's but seems more attuned to empty spaces.

ANOTHER UNUSUAL BIRD of the mountains with many folk-names is the Capercailzie. This is the largest member of the Grouse family and cock birds can weigh 8 kg – about the same as a medium-sized Christmas turkey. Its name derives from the Gaelic, *'Capulli coille'*, which means 'Horse of the Woods'. Even further back that was *'Ceiliog coed'*. Other ancient names were: Cock of the Mountain, Great Grouse and Grouse of the Forests. Its range extends right across Scandinavia and into Russia way beyond the Ural Mountains and on into Siberia. It used to be hunted in Scotland even though the flesh is very pungent with pine-gum. It feeds on the shoots of pine, spruce and larch. Heavy snow in these northern areas does not worry the bird, but in winter it may come down from the forests into open fields to forage on turnips and potatoes.

March

THE BLACK GROUSE is another member of the family *Tetraonidae* adapted to northern moors and forests. Its range worldwide is about the same as the Capercailzie, although extending further east in Russia, almost to the Pacific. The cock is called 'The Dandy of the North'; with glossy blue-black plumage and tail fanned like a big white rose, bordered by crescent-shaped black feathers, and head adorned with a coronet of red inflatable combs, the males gather at traditional places called *leks* from autumn to summer. On these lekking grounds they show off their plumage to each other while performing ritual dances.

THE BLACK GROUSE's tail feathers are greatly prized by hunters (they are often used to adorn the hats of Tyrolean hunters) and even regimental soldiers. One Scottish regiment has the semi-circular feathers fixed in their bonnets.

HOODED CROWS MAY have eggs this month in the Highlands and northern hills. Their grey backs, wing linings and bellies separate them from Carrion Crows but the two might interbreed successfully.

Sightings

1
....

2
....

3
....

4
....

5
....

6
....

7
....

8
....

9
....

10
....

11
....

12
....

13
....

14
....

March

15
....

16
....

17
....

18
....

19
....

20
....

21
....

22
....

23
....

24
....

25
....

26
....

27
....

28
....

29
....

30
....

31
....

April

Garden Birds

THIS IS ONE of the busiest months in the garden for birds. First chicks of several species may have hatched; unmated males attempt wife-stealing, and incompetent or jealous wives steal nest material.

ALL BIRDS HAVE to somehow keep a wary eye open for Britain's seven million cats, not to speak of marauding Sparrowhawks that will require at least 300 victims each per year. Grey squirrels eat nestlings, while Jays, Crows, Magpies and rats quickly learn which nest is where and the optimum moment to plunder its contents. Dog owners should also keep a close watch on what their four-legged companion is up to when let off the lead.

TODAY IT IS illegal to collect birds' eggs or even to disturb birds at the nest, but years ago it was common (my grandfather had a very extensive collection from which I learnt a great deal). Green eggs marbled with brown belong to Blackbirds; Song Thrushes lay blue eggs speckled with black; House Sparrows pale grey marbled with dark grey; Dunnocks and Starlings lay eggs that are pale blue; Magpies and Rooks green marbled with grey; Pigeons, Owls, Nuthatches, Kingfishers pure white; Chaffinches dull white blotched by black and red; Robins cream with ginger speckles.

April

916,000 Blackcap Warblers return early this month from the western Mediterranean to nest in Britain, many of them in rural gardens. They sing lustily with a bright and breezy song. The male with his black skull-cap may build three or four cock nests advertising his suitability as a mate for the female with her brown cap. She will choose one of the nests and furnish it with softer material such as fine grass and animal hair.

Depending of course on what your neighbours do and your own surrounding habitat, rule of thumb suggests a successful bird garden has breeding pairs of Dunnock, Song Thrush, Great Tit, Chaffinch, Bullfinch and Wren – at the very least, Robin, Blackbird and Blue Tit.

Old apple trees provide lichens that grow on the branches for Chaffinch and Long-tailed Tit nest building. A Chaffinch in Norwich is known to have used confetti from a churchyard in lieu of lichen to adorn the outside of its cup nest! Long-tailed Tits will line their long, dome-shaped nests with up to 2,000 feathers.

The noise of the dawn chorus should keep you awake this month and next: enjoy. Tell those who complain that a silent spring indicates a damaged environment – and that might also spell trouble for humans too.

Woodland

Cuckoo! Cuckoo! Three cheers,
And let the welkin ring.
He has not folded wing,
Since last he saw Algiers.

From 'Clevedon Verses', T. E. Brown

BIRDSONG WILL BE in full chorus by the end of
the month. First to begin are Blackbirds and Song
Thrushes which may drown out the smaller birds –
Great Tits and Blue Tits start half an hour later. Each
male sings to keep out rivals, so the louder the better.
Every singer has his prominent perch from which to
announce his right to territory, but he will also have
several other song posts and will circulate around
these throughout the day well into the summer.

OAK, ALDER AND birch forests on the west of Britain,
especially Wales, have Pied Flycatchers arriving from
Africa to breed. Old Woodpecker holes used to be
favourite nest holes but (sign of the times!) nowadays
they prefer nest boxes. The males are conspicuously
black and white and sing loudly from mid April. The
female is pale brown with a white chest and wing
bars. As she carries dead oak leaves, bracken
fibres, rootlets and grass to make
her nest, he may pursue her, making
explosive chattering.

ANOTHER WOODLAND MIGRANT seeking tree holes is the Redstart – but it needs entrance holes 2 inches (50 mm) wide. The male has a rambling twittering song, which can be heard up to 400 metres away. Both sexes have orange-brown rumps. Old names were Bob-tail and Fire-tail.

NIGHTINGALES START ARRIVING on the south coast in the first week of April. Up to 5,000 pairs breed with us across the south-east. Did one ever sing in Berkeley Square? Unlikely. The bird needs scattered trees, especially oak, with thick shrub layer untouched by deer because the nest is on or nearly on the ground, made of oak leaves layered rather like the leaves of a cabbage.

WILLOW AND GRASSHOPPER Warblers may arrive by the end of March but mainly at the beginning of April on the south coast; Garden Warblers usually a day or two later. Willow Warblers have a beautiful falling cadence; Grasshoppers an endless whirr like a sewing machine; Garden Warblers a lovely babble of mellow notes.

ONE OF THE most difficult songs to hear of woodland birds is that of the Treecreeper: nothing more than a weak, high-pitched, *'cheep-cheep-cheep-chizzy-cheep'*. They nest behind loose bark on large old damaged trees or in larch-lap when this starts to peel.

Wetland and Coastal

MOST WINTERING BIRDS will now have
left for the north, though non-breeding
waders or late arrivals can still fill your day
on the estuaries. Many will be changing
plumage: Godwits once grey become
rufous; Sanderlings and Dunlin grow rusty
backs as do others in the Sandpiper family.
Dunlin grow a big black patch on the belly.
Turnstones become harlequins with more buff-chestnut
and black and white.

ONE OF THE most spectacular summer plumage
changes is the Ruff (the male), though his mate (the
reeve) remains dull brown. Ruffs grow long ear tufts
and neck feathers, which they erect and puff out on
the breeding or lekking grounds in the Fens and east
coast marshes. Each bird has its own special colour
coding which may be brick red, glossy black, white or
combinations of all these.

THE SEA CLIFFS around Britain now become crowded
with sea birds returning to breed. Flamborough
Head in Yorkshire is now home to 200,000 sea birds.
Gannets, Kittiwakes, Fulmars and Herring Gulls
nest on the cliff ledges and will be there until
late September.

April

FIVE THOUSAND PUFFINS return to the sea cliffs on
Skomer Island in the Irish Sea just off the coast of
Wales: even more (70,000) on St Kilda, and other
islands such as Isle of May, and at Foula, Sule Skerry
and Fair Isle. These are cold-water ocean birds which
only come ashore, rather clumsily like other deep-sea
birds, to breed, mainly in rabbit holes.

FROM EVEN FARTHER south now come the terns to
breed around our shores: Common, Arctic, Roseate,
Sandwich and Little Terns start to arrive on the south
coast from late March to late April. Many people
cannot tell Common and Arctic apart, so these are
known as 'comic terns'.

INLAND LAKES AND old gravel pits, town ponds and
city lakes will usually have Canada Geese, perhaps
fighting Mallard and even Swans for territory.
Introduced 250 years ago from North America for
ornamental purposes, they have become rather a pest,
fouling water and creating problems for our native
water creatures.

THIS MONTH SEARCH larger lakes for the Great
Crested Grebe. They have grown large orange-
coloured ruffs round their necks and display these
to each other while presenting a piece of water weed
as a wedding gift to one another. They
stand upright on the surface during this
touching but comical ceremony, reaching
up as high as they can to touch beaks.

Field and Farm

'If it thunders
on All Fools' Day
It brings good crops of corn and hay.'

WATCH THE FIELD fences for migrants passing through. Whinchats, Wheatears, Stonechats and even the occasional Hoopoe are wire-perchers. These migrants will use the same throughways along valleys year after year as they travel north.

THE OLD NAME for Wheatear was 'White Arse', because of its distinctive white rump patch. They arrive in March–April, spreading north to breed. In the Victorian era 12,000 were often netted in one day at Brighton for the London restaurant market.

ROOKS HAVE SUCH a well-developed sense of community their gatherings are known as 'Rook Parliaments'. Certainly they watch their neighbours' business as much as their own and make plenty of comment with continual cawing even on moonlit nights. Although they usually break off new twigs from the tips of boughs to build their nests, they will steal each other's sticks if they think they can get away with it.

FIELDFARES CONTINUE MOVING east as the month continues. They will have a favourite April tree where before dusk they gather, sometimes in hundreds, making a clattering chorus of song and chatter. But if the local farm cropping changes from stock to arable, the ancient meeting tree will be abandoned.

April

WHITETHROAT WARBLERS NEST in thick farmland hedges, especially if there is bramble. First arrivals on the south coast may be in the last days of March. Their jerky upward display flight and scratchy song are as distinctive as their pale grey throat feathers looking like a powder puff. They overwinter in the Sahel region of Africa and suffer spectacular population crashes if drought and overgrazing combine in that vulnerable desert area.

PONDS NEEDED FOR cart and carriage horses were once common to every farm and large house and were nesting places for Moorhens and Mallard, although the eggs were taken for the table. But these ponds also need to be provided with good bush cover round them for protection and shelter for nesting; or provide some nesting boxes. Moorhen chicks, with their prickly black down and red beaks, are great fun to watch. The first-generation young will often feed their younger siblings when those hatch out in June.

IF NO PONDS are available then in dry weather Swallows and House Martins will be greatly helped if you place a pan of water for them near soil so that they can make mud bricks to build their nests.

Moor and Mountain

IN APRIL THE hills come alive with the return of summer breeders. Waders such as Dunlin, Golden Plover, Curlew, Common Sandpiper and Greenshank may go no further north in spring than the Welsh mountains, even Dartmoor in Devon. More go over the border into southern Scotland, while the majority go right up into Lapland, and all stations in-between.

ONE OF THE most thrilling sounds in the northern hemisphere's natural world is the spring song of the Curlew. They trill their long, liquid bubbles of song at dawn on luminous northern midsummer nights, during moonlight and at dusk, and also in damp occluded weather. First eggs can be laid at the beginning of April but more likely in the middle of the month.

SHORT-EARED OWLS RETURN from the coasts and lower marshes in March and by early April will have made their nests on the moorlands and mountains of northern England and as far north as the Shetlands. They hunt by day as well as by night and are easily recognised by their long, narrow wings and small head. This owl has a habit of staring at you with its large yellow eyes as it flies past.

April

GOLDEN EAGLES CAN be seen up to a mile away as they soar on their 7-foot (2.3-metre) wings. Usually two eggs are laid, which are heavily blotched with rusty marks over dull white, and are around 7.5 cm in length. Capercailzie's eggs are quite small in comparison, being about the size of a decent hen's egg. Unlike most birds, Golden Eagles seldom lay replacement eggs. It is forbidden to approach these nests, of course.

THERE MAY BE snow on the Highlands in April where the Red Grouse (unique to Britain) is nesting. Eggs might be badly frosted but they will usually hatch out quite successfully.

MERLIN RETURN TO the Highlands, but eggs are not laid until next month. Some birds have wandered southward in winter as far as the tropics. The male weighs only 4 ounces and is only one third the length of a Golden Eagle. Its name comes from the ancient German *smiril*, then old French *esmirrillon*.

GOLDEN PLOVER LAY their first eggs mid month. The males fight with raised wings and leapfrog over their rivals and may chase several females. Their liquid song with mournful, penetrating calls gives the wild spirit of the lonely moors almost as strongly as the call of the Curlew.

Sightings

1
....

2
....

3
....

4
....

5
....

6
....

7
....

8
....

9
....

10
....

11
....

12
....

13
....

14
....

15 ....

16 ....

17 ....

18 ....

19 ....

20 ....

21 ....

22 ....

23 ....

24 ....

25 ....

26 ....

27 ....

28 ....

29 ....

30 ....

May

Garden

Blackcap, Blackcap,
What delight you're bringing –
Singing, Singing
That joyous roundelay!

MAY DAY IS *the* day to get up for the dawn chorus,
even if only in your own garden.

YOU ARE NOT allowed by law to disturb nests, but it
is inevitable that some which are low down allow a
quick look as you pass by. Perhaps the most beautiful
of all the small garden birds' eggs belong to the
Dunnock. They are blue like polished turquoise, and
lie in a cup of green moss which resembles velvet.

PIED WAGTAILS THRIVE near buildings and will often
nest on them, especially if there is water nearby, and
the buildings are old with nest crevices. Old names are
Dishwasher, Nanny Washtail, Wagster, Washerwoman.
Their speckled grey eggs will hatch mid month when the
parents will be very busy keeping the flies down around
your property.

May

THE CHEEKY HOUSE Sparrow has greatly declined in recent years, but if you are lucky to have them near, watch how the cock birds display their black throats as they surround a hen bird.

ALTHOUGH NOT STRICTLY garden birds, many Swifts nest in the roofs of country houses and overfly gardens from about 4 May when they arrive from Africa. They require gaps in soffit and barge boards in gable ends to enable them to get under the tiles to make a nest; this is the most amazing sight. Be aware: your home improvements could make them homeless.

BLUE TITS SING throughout the day, a very high tinkling song, the repetition of three notes. They breed early but often lose the first brood due to bad weather or predation, and so could be laying a second set of eggs.

ROBINS ALSO HAVE hungry offspring to feed and will be grateful for any worms you turn up as you weed your flower beds, as will the Blackbirds.

YOU MAY HAVE Starlings nesting in your disused chimney pot. They are lively, comical birds – not black, as some think; look closely and you will see their plumage has a lovely iridescent purple, blue and green sheen together with speckles of white and silver, buff and yellow. Their song is full of mimicry: catcalls, mews of passing gulls, even a chainsaw buzz has been heard.

Woodland

'The green earth, the wind among
the trees, the songs of birds...'

Nature Near London, Richard Jefferies

IN WRITER RICHARD Jefferies' time, during Queen
Victoria's reign, the woodland dawn chorus was at its
height in early June. Nowadays early May is the best time.

DAWN CHORUS IN Caithness, Scotland, is one hour and
ten minutes before Lands End, Cornwall. Strangely, due
to a diagonal movement of sunrise, Clacton in Essex
and Glasgow on the west coast of Scotland experience
sunrise midway between these two extremes. Sunrise
given in diaries is that for Greenwich, London, so some
local adjustment is necessary.

INSECT-EATERS AND BIRDS with large eyes tend to be
among the first songsters. Woodland birds in Britain
usually start singing in this order: Blackbird, Song
Thrush, Pheasant, Crow, Wood Pigeon. The second group
roughly in this order: Robin, Redstart, Garden Warbler,
Blackcap, Mistle Thrush, Willow Warbler, Wren, Great
Tit, Chiffchaff, Great Spotted Woodpecker,
Blue Tit, Green Woodpecker, Chaffinch,
Nuthatch, Whitethroat and Treecreeper.

THE WHISTLING, SQUEAKING, squawking jumble of sound may seem impossible to disentangle into individual songs, but can be achieved quite quickly by total concentration – or you can just give yourself up to enjoy the chaotic cacophony.

RECENTLY CLEARED WOODLANDS and young pine plantations may be the habitat for the Grasshopper Warbler. This secretive little brown bird behaves like a mouse – its nest is often on the ground or about half a metre above in dense tussocks of grass and bramble. Both male and female birds approach the nest by using a hidden path under dense vegetation. The male sings his mechanical reeling sewing-machine-like note for hours on end, especially on moonlit nights.

BIRDS WHICH REMAIN hidden as they sing or concealed by darkness, such as the Nightingale or Nightjar, can afford long stretches of song without being discovered by predators. Birds which perch openly, such as Chaffinch and Wren, can only allow short bursts of song; they have to pause, look round for predators, and move to a fresh song-perch.

GREAT SPOTTED WOODPECKERS use percussion instead of song. The instrument is a thin dead branch at the top of a tree which the male strikes up to twenty times in three quarters of a second giving a drum roll heard half a mile (almost a kilometre) away.

Wetland and Coastal

THE GARGANEY IS one of Britain's rarest breeding ducks. Up to a hundred pairs fly 3,000 miles from Equatorial Africa to breed in fens, damp meadows and marshes. They are called Summer Teal, and are about the same size as the Teal. The male has a large white eye-stripe. Old names were Pied Wigeon and Cricket Teal, because the male has a croaking call in the breeding season. Many RSPB wetland sites in lowland England protect them, but they are very secretive and difficult to see except when several males chase a single female, chirping like crickets.

SHELDUCK NEST DOWN rabbit burrows. These can often be miles from water on downland or farmland, so the ducklings are led in a gang sometimes for miles to the nearest river or beach and many perish en route.

THE LITTLE GREBE (Dabchick) – pale yellow beak spot, chestnut-red throat – has a shrill ringing call in the breeding season.

WATER RAILS ALMOST look like small Moorhens but are hardly ever seen. You are more likely to hear them growling, whistling, squeaking, grunting, groaning and screaming like a pig.

May

MARSH HARRIERS HAVE spread widely across East Anglia, due to protection and publicity by the RSPB and other similar groups. The females and juveniles' buff crown gave them the old names of White-headed Harpy and Bald Buzzard. During courtship the male performs a spectacular 70-metre dive complete with rolls and somersaults.

SEARCH THE QUIET shady lakes and old gravel pits for the Gadwall Duck. These are overall dull brown but have an unmistakable black under-tail, which you can see easily with binoculars 100 metres away. Their breeding stronghold in Scotland is Loch Leven; specimens here may be descendants of the original true native stock. Farther south the stock is largely descended from two birds caught at a Norfolk duck decoy (a long net tunnel into which duck are enticed) in 1850.

GOLDENEYE DUCKS NEST inside Woodpecker holes in pine trees; flying into the holes at 40 mph, braking by hitting the sides with outstretched wings. Ouch!

TERNS (COMMON, LITTLE, SANDWICH) lay between two and four eggs each on sea (and sometimes inland lake) beaches. Famous colonies are Blakeney Point and Scolt Head Island on the north coast of Norfolk. They are very vulnerable to predation by foxes, gulls, stoats and sadly, dogs. But all colonies are also prone to sudden abandonment: even a thousand birds flying away for no known reason.

Field and Farm

NEARLY TWO MILLION Skylarks will be singing this month and on into July around the whole country. You will need to be out in the cornfields long before dawn to hear their very first song at around 2.30 a.m. You won't see them then, for they will be under the stars, but this can be a magical experience.

LESSER WHITETHROATS ARE difficult to see but not to hear. The song can be heard half a mile (almost a kilometre) away; a very loud, rattling trill. There are about 60,000 pairs breeding in Britain, only one tenth the number of Common Whitethroats. Lesser Whitethroats have just that – less of a white throat – are a slightly smaller size, black legs instead of pale brown, and darker back. Their habitat preference is scattered trees and overgrown hedges with brambles, typically along old lanes and bridleways.

LOW-LYING FARM FIELDS and meadows with drainage ditches can be havens for Reed and Sedge Warblers. These summer migrants don't necessarily need wetlands in which to breed: drainage ditches with reeds will do.

HOUSE MARTINS OFTEN find nesting habitat around farm buildings: fragile mud cups stuck onto walls, which are very liable to takeover by Sparrows. Why not put up House Martin nesting boxes as they do in Portugal? These are small fibreglass cups that are an enormous help to these birds.

SAND MARTINS HAVE suffered recent decline due to loss of habitat (sandy cliffs, quarries). Artificial wooden imitation cliffs with nest-holes are now made to compensate.

MAGPIE NESTS ARE built like fortresses. The cup for the eggs and young is a thick foundation of hard mud cemented to twigs. This is lined with fine roots. The cup is then guarded by a cage of thick twigs, which will keep out any unwanted predators. This bird of course is busy taking the eggs and chicks of smaller birds for its own use.

CIRL BUNTINGS, WHICH are close relatives of Yellowhammers, have been successfully conserved by the RSPB on farmland in south Devon, where less than 100 breed. First noticed there 200 years ago, it is on the northern edge of its range and was hit by hard winters in the past.

CAN YOU TELL a Tree Sparrow from a House Sparrow? Tree Sparrows have a chestnut crown and black cheek spot; House have a grey crown and no spot. Tree Sparrow sexes look similar, unlike the House, and they like to be near trees, especially in suburbia.

Moor and Mountain

THE SONG OF the Capercailzie lasts only five seconds, but is repeated over and over again, sometimes until nearly midday. The black tail is fanned upright, the wings clapped, and the head held erect as the cock delivers his challenge from a clearing in the forests of the north. The song starts with an accelerating *'t'kup, t'kup, tuk-tuk-tuk'* followed with a loud pop like a champagne cork exploding, ending with a conspiratorial whisper. The whole performance is blatant showing off, unafraid because the bird is big enough to have few, if any, predators. Like the Pheasant, the cock will often challenge a passing forest vehicle.

WHIMBRELS LOOK LIKE slightly smaller Curlews. About 400 breeding pairs lay their first eggs at the end of May on moors and exposed heathlands of Shetland. They were once called Titterels, or Seven Whistlers, because that was the sound of their song. Scottish names were Land Whaap or Little Whaap.

SNOW BUNTINGS ARE one of the last birds to lay eggs as they nest on the highest parts of the Scottish mountains, the Grampians and north-west Highlands. The old name for them was Snowflake, which describes how they look as they fly in parties across the tops. Another name, Great Pied Mountain Finch, describes what they look like. Up to eight eggs are laid in a deep cup of dead grass and roots, lined with fine grass, wool and feathers if obtainable.

SIX HUNDRED AND fifty pairs of Dotterel should have arrived on the mountains from wintering grounds around the Mediterranean. These small Plovers used to be very much more common but were hunted almost to extinction because they are so tame. The female is brighter coloured than the male – she does the courting – and having laid the eggs leaves him to hatch them and look after the young. Females have been known to then migrate further north to Norway and find another male, who will rear a second family for her.

HEN HARRIERS MAY breed in the Cambrian Mountains of north Wales but more likely in Islay, Jura, and Cromarty in Scotland. There are about 5,000 pairs in Western Europe and 10 per cent of those are in the UK.

ONE OF THE most thrilling sights in birdwatching is to see a male passing food to a female on the wing. Also the male performing his corkscrewing courting aerobatics, swooping, somersaulting, stalling and diving out with closed wings.

Sightings

1

2

3

4

5

6

7

8

9

10

11

12

13

14

15
....

16
....

17
....

18
....

19
....

20
....

21
....

22
....

23
....

24
....

25
....

26
....

27
....

28
....

29
....

30
....

31
....

June

Garden

NESTLINGS ABOUND! YOUNG birds need protein for body-building, mainly caterpillars, insects and other invertebrates such as earthworms for Robins and Blackbirds.

YOU SHOULD ALREADY have stopped putting out peanuts (they can kill fledglings by choking – think of a human baby). A good mixture is a large spoonful of cottage cheese mixed with plenty of breadcrumbs: soft and damp. Remember to scrub down bird tables regularly to keep avian pox at bay.

VERY SHALLOW WATER trays are especially attractive to young Blue Tits emerging now.

BLACKBIRDS WILL BE starting their second laying of four eggs this month, even a third set by the end. The juveniles of the first brood will still hang around the parents wondering why they are no longer as important as they had thought! Hen Blackbirds may use the old nest if this was a secure and successful location first time round, otherwise she might build another nearby.

June

BULLFINCHES MIGHT ANNOY you by stripping the buds off your apple and pear trees, eating up to 45 in a minute. But remember apple trees can lose half their buds in spring without any serious decline in the amount of fruit (perhaps it is designed that way?). They are very attractive birds to watch, especially the males with bright orange-pink chests, often called 'John Bulls'.

BULLFINCHES ARE BECOMING much less common nowadays. These secretive birds nest in small gardens, if there is some thick cover around. The nest is made of fine twigs crisscrossed onto the twigs of a shrub such as ivy, privet, yew or rhododendron. On this a deep strong cup of rootlets and long hair is woven. The eggs are palest blue with untidy, scattered blotches of deep red.

GOLDFINCHES MAKE VERY small, very neat nests with a secure, deep cup. This is often placed on the last twig of a long apple tree branch, usually well out of human reach. But they can be built up to 40 feet (13 metres) above the ground in a variety of hedgerow trees – hawthorn, elder, even mature trees such as chestnut and lime. You will probably never know they were there until the winter when the nests become visible.

LINNETS WILL SOMETIMES nest in large gardens, especially if there is a sun trap formed by an old wall or a bank of shrubs facing south. Many old names are known – Red-headed Finch, Whinbird, Greater Redpoll, Lintie and Linwhite.

Woodland

BIRDSONG FADES DURING the month of June. Nightingales and Cuckoos stop completely by about the tenth in the south, though some may last another week. Greenfinches, Yellowhammers and Bullfinches sing more. Pheasants keep crowing to the middle of the month. The main burst of territorial song during the warm days is from Wood Pigeons, which will sing on now into early autumn.

LISTEN OUT IN the conifer woods through central and eastern Britain for the un-oiled gate squeak made by hungry Long-eared Owl juveniles. These birds are under-recorded but there may be 2,000 or more pairs altogether.

TAWNY OWL YOUNGSTERS are often found on the ground this month having clambered out of their nests while impatiently waiting for their parents to return with food. They look like a bundle of grey angora wool. They are of course very vulnerable to predators: foxes, badgers – and your dog. If you happen to spot one in distress, place it carefully into a nearby tree or strong bushy shrub, but avoid their claws.

YOU CAN TELL which woodpecker is in the woods by the size of the entrance hole to the nest. Greens are 2½ inches (6 cm); Great Spotted 2 inches (5 cm); Lesser Spotted 1½ inches (3.6 cm). Greens have circular entrances, both spotted woodpeckers are very slightly broader at the base. However, the sight and sound of the birds themselves might be an easier way to tell the difference!

SPARROWHAWKS MIGHT LAY again this month, if eggs or young have been lost. The nests were built in early spring but not used until April. You might easily mistake a Sparrowhawk's nest for that of a Jay or Wood Pigeon, but the twigs will usually be laid all one way, and fall untidily over the side.

HOBBY FALCONS MAY use this year's crows' nests (already finished with) but will throw out the old lining. They will only nest in dense woods if there are plenty of wide rides and glades along which they can catch large butterflies and dragonflies – and insect-hunting House Martins. You can tell a Hobby from a Kestrel by its more streamlined wings and outline like a large Swift – an anchor flashing across the sky.

IF YOU SEE an old nest on the edge of a wood adorned with scraps of paper and all kinds of rubbish, then chances are you are looking at the nest of a Red Kite.

CHIFFCHAFFS KEEP SINGING their name with a second brood. They usually nest slightly above ground level, while Wood Warblers nest on the ground, and Willow Warblers in a hollow in the ground.

Wetland and Coastal

KINGFISHERS WILL START second broods this month. The birds quarry a circular hole about 1½ – 4 feet (0.5 m–3.5 m) in length into a small sandy cliff on a river or lake bank, in which are laid between five and eight eggs at the far end. The entrance hole is foul with droppings and fish bones. Rats, or even House Martins, nesting in a similar location have oval entrance holes. Unlike most, Kingfisher eggs are almost spherical and are bright shiny white.

FRESH AND SALT marshes are now noisy with the piping of worried parent birds trying to warn their young and each other of predators. The waders with young include Redshank, Lapwing, Ringed Plover, Avocet, Oystercatcher and Black-tailed Godwit.

THE FIVE SPECIES of breeding terns nesting on flat sand shores or seaside rocks will often band together and dive repeatedly onto a person's head, sometimes drawing blood as they peck at speed. They will also surround a passing Hawk, Falcon or Skua, like a swarm of bees, and escort the enemy well clear of the ternery.

ON OR JUST after Midsummer's Day, you may see small flocks or 'deserts' – the old word for a group – of Lapwings arriving on the east coast. These are birds and their young that have bred in the Baltic regions and are already coming back west for the winter.

BLACK-HEADED GULLS ACROSS Britain could be brooding their second clutches. About 150,000 pairs nest in coastal marshes, sand dunes, reservoirs, lakes and tarns in Scotland. In the breeding season their velvet chocolate heads contrast wonderfully well with their cherry red beaks and legs. They build chunky nests on salt marshes, or sketchy grass and rubbish nests in sand dunes – occasionally they will build up to 20 feet up in a tree.

KITTIWAKE EGGS ARE hatching now; they are the daintiest gull of all breeding in Britain. But their numbers have halved in the past ten years down to 200,000, due to sea warming and decline in sand eels. One colony thriving, though, is in Sussex at Splash Point, Seaford, an RSPB reserve on the chalk cliffs. At their old stronghold in the Orkneys and Shetland they were once called Waeg, Annet, Tarrock and Mackerel bird.

COMMON GUILLEMOTS BREEDING around the rocky coasts of Britain are also called Murres – because the sound of a colony busily looking after the young and all birds talking together is known as 'murring'.

Field and Farm

WOOD PIGEONS CAN have five separate broods in one year, totalling ten eggs altogether, although the first two are often unsuccessful. An adult can live for over ten years, and may well hold the same territory all that time. If you listen carefully you can tell one male from another, as the calls of separate birds, although basically similar in syllable and phrasing, all have very slightly different tone and inflection.

SWIFT EGGS HATCH mid month. The nest is often nothing more than a collection of dust and spiders' webs but some birds glue small pieces of dead grass together with feathers collected aerially with their saliva. By the end of the month hungry young swifts make such a noise after daybreak as to wake cottage dwellers with open windows under the eaves.

THE CORN BUNTING is one of the few birds that does not fully retract its legs as it flies. Its song, heard among cornfields with scattered hedgerows, is described as a bunch of keys being jangled.

HOLLOW HEDGEROW TREES (usually old ash) are one of the safest places for the Kestrel to nest. Failing those, this small falcon will find an old squirrel's drey, crow's nest, or church tower. They are very useful to the farmer in keeping down mice.

June

YOUNG ROOKS HAVE now flown the nest. Until only 40 years ago, they were harvested by farmers as the birds sat among the tree branches. Rook pie was a luxury for farm-workers' families.

THE WIDE OPEN fields of central England are the main breeding areas of Quail. The ventriloqual call of the male *'wit, wit-wit'* (or 'wet-my-lips') can be heard a mile away. Some years over a thousand pairs migrate here from Africa, flying in at night. Normally only a few hundred reach our shores. Up to 13 eggs are laid. Quails were netted for food across Europe until they became protected in 1937. Beethoven included the Quail's song together with that of the Nightingale and Cuckoo at the end of the second movement of his Pastoral Symphony (No. 6).

THE WOODLARK'S SONG, which will end mid month, is so beautiful as to be thought second only to the Nightingale. In France it is called 'Lulu', which describes the lilting falling cadence. Numbers are increasing but only 1,500 pairs nest, in Cornwall, Hampshire, Sussex and East Anglia, where scattered trees for song posts and dry, rough heathland, cleared woodlands or derelict pastures are found.

Moor and Mountain

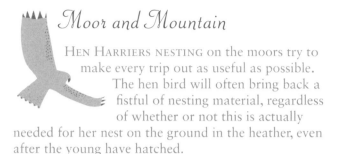

HEN HARRIERS NESTING on the moors try to make every trip out as useful as possible. The hen bird will often bring back a fistful of nesting material, regardless of whether or not this is actually needed for her nest on the ground in the heather, even after the young have hatched.

KESTRELS NEST ON moorland as well as southern woodland and farmland. On cragless mountains they will nest on the ground in dense heather. In these situations the birds will make a tunnel through the heather stems and be completely hidden from view. Four to six eggs are covered with dense red-brown blotches and resemble small Peregrine eggs.

SONG THRUSHES ARE another moorland breeder which have to nest on the ground in dense heather, especially in the Hebrides.

RING OUZELS PREFER something slightly different with their moorland nests. These are often in clumps of bulging vegetation such as bracken, bilberry, woodrush or grass clumps overhanging a stream bank, the top of an old mine shaft or quarry. However, some birds just nest inside a nook of a dry stone wall. Birds (returning from Mediterranean countries) are often faithful to the same nest site for several years.

June

WHINCHATS ARE SLIGHTLY smaller than Robins and less obvious in their cinnamon plumage, but the male does have a prominent white eye-strip and blackish cheek, which might catch your eye. On moorland in Wales and Scotland you will hear the cock bird singing before you see him. The brief bright warble sometimes has mimics of other birds' songs. Young conifer plantations under ten feet in height often provide a good habitat.

STONECHATS HAVE A squeaky song as they dance up and down in flight showing off their black, white and orange plumage to their mates. Nests are built typically in isolated gorse bushes. Their call, which resembles two stones being hit together, can be heard up to half a mile (almost a kilometre) away. This gave them lots of old country names such as Stone Chatterer, Stoneclink, Stone Smick, Fuzz Chat (Furze – i.e. gorse) and Stone Chucker.

DIPPERS NEST OVER moorland streams, often behind waterfalls, and are now beginning their second broods. The nest is domed – bigger than a Wren's – of brown moss, lined with dead oak or birch leaves. They nest early because they have not had to migrate and have built up plenty of body fat by fishing underwater for shrimps and larvae, having had this luxurious feast all to themselves.

Sightings

1 ....

2 ....

3 ....

4 ....

5 ....

6 ....

7 ....

8 ....

9 ....

10 ....

11 ....

12 ....

13 ....

14 ....

June

15
....

16
....

17
....

18
....

19
....

20
....

21
....

22
....

23
....

24
....

25
....

26
....

27
....

28
....

29
....

30
....

July

Garden

SOME OF YOUR garden birds will now be bringing their families to your feeding station: others will disperse in social flocks. Blue Tits often rear young in a colony and so two or three families can descend in a crowd, especially to bathe in the bird bath. Young Blue Tits are slightly yellower than their blue parents. The inexperienced juveniles might easily drown if the water is more than an inch deep.

MOST YOUNG STARLINGS behave like rowdy teenagers, demanding food and attention from their parents. They will all come down onto the lawn to follow the old birds hunting for insects and worms. They are mouse brown with a whiter throat than their iridescent parents, and their legs and beaks are blackish. Parents have almost reddish-brown legs. Family parties gang together early in the month and string out along telegraph wires like the notes of a lively song.

YOUNG ROBINS HAVE speckled breasts. They are being taught the sounds of communication they will need later in life by their fathers, whose song is now slightly different to that of the spring. Young Robins will start to reply before the month is out.

MOST OTHER GARDEN birds will have more or less stopped singing by the end of the month, but Greenfinches will outlast the song of the Chaffinch and may even start a third brood.

BULLFINCHES ARE NOW feeding the caterpillars off your fruit trees to their young.

MANY YOUNG BIRDS wanting adventure (as is the wont of the young!) stray from the family flock and will pay a heavy price for it. They are the ones which feed the predators – that also have young to feed. But over-adventurous young can with luck be the ones which pioneer mass invasions. Sixty years ago Collared Doves were found to have travelled up to 500 miles westward from their traditional breeding areas in just one year to start new colonies in Britain.

PARTIES OF YOUNG Swifts race at breakneck speed through the rooftops, apparently screaming with the thrill of flying after being shut in their dark, dusty eave-nests. But the screaming is actually a way of keeping together. Old names for them included 'Screech Martin' and 'Devil Bird'. Nearly every Swift will have left in the last few days of the month. They will not land on the ground or a building again until next May when they return to their nests.

Woodland

JULY HAS ALWAYS been known as the 'Silent Month' in the countryside, as many birds start to moult. Years ago schoolchildren used to collect these feathers and stick them into books – a lot was learnt about birds in that way.

HOBBY FALCONS ARE now rearing their young in southern England. They will bring back solid protein in the form of young Swallows, Martins, Larks and Pipits and also large insects. The male sometimes makes an aerial pass of food to the female or he will land in a nearby tree and call her off the nest to come and eat. A parent bird returning to the nest may 'stoop' from a great height straight to the ground, only pulling back up at the very last split second.

CARRION CROWS SOMETIMES join forces into huge family flocks, which might make you think that they are Rooks instead. As many as 300 Crows can be recorded together now in one large flock known as a 'murder of Crows'.

MAGPIES OFTEN MIMIC Buzzards and Sparrowhawks to warn their young of these predators. Hungry juvenile Magpies sit in the shade in deep cover, calling continuously and raucously for food. The adults lose their tail feathers from now on and may look very odd as they flutter across the sky.

WRENS CONTINUE TO sing with a second burst of activity now and they will build more of their featherless nests for the hen to inspect and possibly choose for her second brood. Some nests are built inside old Magpie nests or the bird might attach it onto that of an old Dipper's nest by a stream. Back in the freezing winter of 1963, 79 per cent of Wrens were killed by the deep and prolonged cold. Six years later their numbers were back to normal.

WOOD WARBLERS ARE gradually moving their range northwards, even into the Shetlands. Their habitat requirement is for dense woodland with branches on trees close to the ground and with 70 per cent shade to protect nests from sunlight.

ONE OF THE most difficult birds to see, despite its brilliant plumage of yellow and black, is the Golden Oriole. Only about 30 nest in Britain, in dense woodland canopy mainly in the Fens where poplars grow, but they could be found in any dense woodland. A loud squawk or more often a simple fluting whistle like a Blackbird beginner may give it away but the bird hardly ever shows itself.

Wetland and Coastal

BIRDERS WATCH THE east coast landfall sites avidly from now on as waders and passerines (perching birds) start the south-westward autumn migration. The north Norfolk coast has RSPB, National Trust and Natural England nature reserves with visitor access. One of the most famous is Cley Marshes owned by Norfolk Wildlife Trust. Reed beds alternate with grazing marshes and freshwater pools, holding countless thousands of migratory and resident birds and the list of rarities recorded is very impressive.

MOORHENS LIVING ON town ponds are often quite tame so you can watch their unusual family life close by. Older female chicks hatched in April and now almost full grown will feed baby siblings hatched in July. The mother bird will feed both sets.

DON'T SNIFF AT sewage farms as wetland sites until you've seen the great variety of birds they can attract. They are good places to see both Common and Green Sandpipers arriving this month, which feed on the flies.

JULY SEES CONTINUATION of the four Shearwater species as they move south along the east coast. Cory's, Sooty, Manx and Balearic are dark brown, long-winged, deep ocean gliders which almost look as swift and sure as Peregrines.

THOSE 'WHITE MICE' of the mudflat tide-lines – Dunlin – arrive in thousands from the north. Look carefully: you might be seeing the Southern form from south-east Greenland and Iceland; the Greenland form from north-east Greenland; the Northern form from Russia; or even one from North America and Siberia (but that is very rare).

TERNS MAY LAY repeat clutches of eggs if the high tides washed away the first eggs and young. In Scotland, the Common and Arctic Tern nest up to 1,200 feet (400 m). Both parents and young have to fight off their neighbours when food is brought home. Young are often killed in such battles.

ROSEATE TERNS ARE now down to less than a hundred pairs in Britain, plus a few hundred in Ireland.

A FEW HUNDRED pairs of Little Egrets breed in southern Britain in coastal woodland. The ground beneath the colony (called a rookery) is a mess of whitewash, broken eggs, white feathers and even the occasional dead bird not yet cleared up by foxes.

YOUNG CHOUGHS LEAVE the rocky coastal breeding grounds, staying with their parents in family parties. The nests they were reared in are much neater than those of close cousins the Jackdaw and are made of heather, gorse, grass, wool and feathers.

Field and Farm

Two hundred and forty years ago Gilbert White – Britain's first systematic recorder of wildlife events – noted that the first hay-day in the countryside was also that day when the young Swallows took their first flights: in early July. Today meadows are mown in May, but the Swallows still fly at the same time; Sand Martins a few days earlier; Swifts and House Martins by the middle of July.

FARMERS IN EAST Anglian breckland have collaborated with the RSPB in helping to protect most of England's 165 pairs of Stone Curlew on their land, sadly in decline elsewhere. By July, gatherings of young and their parents feed in arable fields. Stone Curlew belong to the family 'Thick-knees'. Their wild cries at night on lonely fields gave them the name of 'the Shepherd's Friend', and they are also known as the 'Norfolk Plover'. You can watch this rather strange Plover with its big, sad-looking, yellow eyes from hides at RSPB reserves.

CHARMS (GATHERINGS OR flocks) of Goldfinches, normally secretive, will now be searching the hedgerows and fields for the first thistle seeds. Their most popular old name was King Harry, others included Goldspink, Thistle-finch, Redcap and Proud-tail.

YOUNG CROWS TAKE just over a month (30–35 days) to become airborne after hatching. So some will still be in their nests, begging for food with hungry calls, in the first week of the month.

BARN OWLS TAKE even longer, the young sometimes not flying for three months after hatching: the egg taking over a month to hatch first. The loud snoring coming from the young in their nest has often worried people, thinking a person was in distress!

CORNCRAKES WERE ONCE common farmland birds, ground-nesters and relying on the hay crop being harvested in July. Modern methods and earlier cutting in May destroys the sitting birds, young and eggs. However, the RSPB have reserves of farmland in Northern Ireland devoted to the ecology of this rarity. It may have second clutches now and on into August. It is related to the Moorhen and Coot, and is sometimes called Landrail. Its call, like a stick drawn across a comb, is called 'crekking' and can be heard half a mile away.

MEADOW PIPITS MAY have third broods in July. Males fly up like Skylarks to sing but only for a few metres before parachuting gently back to the meadow with wings held half open and legs dangling down.

Moor and Mountain

THE COMMONS OF the south, moors of the west and mountains of the north all now begin to bloom purple and red with bell heather and ling. Blaeberries (bilberries) and cranberries begin fruiting and are a source of food together with the myriad invertebrates for those Waders, Plovers, Finches, Pipits, Grouse and Larks, which remain with their young before most drift south at the start of the autumn in August.

FLOCKS OF YOUNG Twites reared in the mountains bounce in exuberant flight, keeping tight together in communal defence against Harriers, Hawks and Falcons. Their strange name reflects their flight call – a nasal *'twayte'*. When they land they hop along the ground looking for weed seeds. They resemble Linnets but are more streaky brown.

UP TO 2,000 pairs of Nightjars still reach this country from Africa to breed. They are related to Swifts. In early summer the males start their churring song at dusk – a magical sound on summer evenings – and continue into July. They used to be called Goatsuckers: a superstitious idea deriving from their habit of taking flies buzzing around the teats of goats and cows – they were not after the animals' milk. The nests are usually in open areas of the heather moors and large forest glades.

ONE OF THE waders which breeds in the Highlands is the Greenshank, once known as 'the long-legged horseman' from its habit of wading up to its belly in the water. A curious unexplained fact about its choice of ground nest site is that it seems to be next to some straight line on the ground. An old peat road, fence-line or ditch, track or even railway line, attracts the female. More naturally, she will nest by a straight line of rock sticking out of the grassland.

PEREGRINES WILL NOW be teaching their youngsters how to catch their own food by bringing home a dead bird, flying past the young who are expecting beak-to-beak feeding, or at least being presented with a ready torn morsel at its feet. Instead the parent drops it in mid-air. The youngsters eventually get the idea and have a go themselves at catching this food – but quite often to begin with dinner falls straight to the ground and stays there.

YOUNG RING OUZELS could be mistaken for Blackbirds because they do not have the white neck crescent or the pale feather edges on flanks which the adult bird has.

Sightings

1

2

3

4

5

6

7

8

9

10

11

12

13

14

July

15
....

16
....

17
....

18
....

19
....

20
....

21
....

22
....

23
....

24
....

25
....

26
....

27
....

28
....

29
....

30
....

31
....

August

Garden

BLACKBIRDS MAY NOW present you with their third broods, which are often the most successful because increased leaf cover has camouflaged their nests from predators.

WELL-WOODED GARDENS WITH old trees surrounding will attract Nuthatches. If so, did you notice their odd nesting habits in the spring? They are unique among British birds for two reasons: they normally line their nests only with strips of pine or birch bark (but failing those, then dead leaves) and they reduce the size of the nest hole in a tree or wall by plastering mud into a circle just wide enough for them to enter.

STILL TIME FOR that rare bird of older gardens, the Spotted Flycatcher, to have young as second broods. If you leave ivy on trees, broken branches still attached to trunks, or have Virginia creeper on the house, these are all natural nest sites. The birds are quite secretive and you may not know they are there until almost before they are due to leave, when their insect-catching behaviour becomes obvious: short flights out and back from their perch.

ANOTHER ODDITY: A female Great Tit may decide to lay her eggs in the nest of a Blue Tit. Being bigger and more dominant, the Great Tit will then find herself having to rear all the young, which could be up to sixteen or more. This is not usual but has been recorded.

TRY GROWING HARDHEADS *(Centaurea nigra)* in your garden borders – the seeds will attract Goldfinches and the flowers are excellent attractions for painted lady butterflies too. Collect some seeds now from wasteland or roadside verges to provide plants for next year.

CHAFFINCHES LEAVE YOUR garden now and join same-sex flocks in the wider countryside.

BLACKBIRDS, DUNNOCKS, SONG Thrushes and Robins sometimes enjoy sunbathing in August on hot tile roofs, or sheltered secluded patches of dry earth, often having had a dust bath first. They stretch their wings out to their fullest extent, raise crests, spread tails, open beaks and go into a delicious stupor as they enjoy a rest. This actually helps rid their feathers of parasites, but they are especially vulnerable to cats.

SONG THRUSHES HUNT for snails in the dry weather and smash the shells on stone anvils, usually on a path. The empty shells mount up over the days and show not just garden snails but the amazing variety of different banded snail colours.

Woodland

' ... IN AUGUST GO he must' the old saying goes for Cuckoos. In fact, that only refers to the youngsters. The parents could leave as early as mid June if the weather has been wet, but normally July. Young Cuckoos are dusky grey-brown with a distinctive white patch on the neck. They might sit around tamely looking a bit like Billy Bunter but they are quick and hawk-like on the wing.

YOUNG GREEN WOODPECKERS call repeatedly during the day now for their parents as they become ever hungrier. Parents have a 75-mm tongue, thin enough to press into ant galleries and extract the adults and larvae. Failing any wood ants or common yellow hill ant castles, or enough beetle larvae in deadwood, the birds may turn to apples, pears, cherries or even acorns.

MANY YOUNG BUZZARDS go hungry now; if food is scarce, earthworms become the diet. The birds might be seen standing on meadows or ploughed fields: sometimes as many as 25 have been seen together in recent years.

ABOUT A DOZEN pairs of Honey Buzzards nest in southern and middle England. They can be distinguished from the Common Buzzard by the longer, narrower tail, which is white beneath with three black bands. Its head is narrower with a longer neck like a pigeon. These very secretive woodland rarities migrate here from Africa and feed mainly on wasp or wild bee larvae.

LIKE THE HARE, the Woodcock has 'eyes in the back of its head'. This means that, unlike most birds, it can literally see behind, because the eyes are set further back than normal, which is very useful as it probes deep into the leaf mould with its long beak, when it might otherwise be surprised by predators.

YOUNG RED KITES will now be quickly learning to patrol roads to search for roadkill.

WOOD PIGEONS MAKE out-and-return flights all day from the woods to harvest fields, bringing home grain and also water for their youngsters which may be 3 miles away from food.

TURTLE DOVES MUCH enjoy the seeds of that agricultural weed – fumitory. Shakespeare maligned the plant as 'rank', an agricultural pest, in *Henry V*, but this is grossly unfair!

PIED FLYCATCHERS IN Welsh and Devon woods are feeding up ready for migration next month. Individuals typically flit out from a perch to catch an insect and at once return, flicking its wings and tail. The call notes are rather like that of a Swallow: *'whit'*.

Wetland and Coastal

THE SOUTHWARD RUSH of birds continues apace from the north in August. In some cases west to east, with vagrant American waders turning up now in lakes and pools on or near the coast. These include White-rumped, Pectoral, and Buff-breasted Sandpipers.

BLACK TERNS NOW arrive in England from breeding on the continent. Good places to see them are on the London reservoirs, Norfolk and Suffolk coasts and inland reservoirs such as Abberton in Essex and Bewl water, Arlington reservoir and Chichester gravel pits in Sussex. Sightings of such rarities can be found on 'Birdline': search online for websites which will give you a local contact telephone number.

YOUNG FULMAR MAY still be in the nest on the cliffs around Britain as they take seven weeks to fledge from hatching. These birds usually live to 25 years of age, but one famous bird called Flora the Fulmar lived to be about 50, having been ringed in the 1950s as an adult and returning to the isle of Eynhallow in the Orkneys in the late 1990s. Fulmar fly with stiff outstretched wings and almost resemble a white Peregrine as they glide back and forth.

STORM PETREL CHICKS are still being fed during the night in their nests on rocky islands of the west and north. Parents coming in under cover of darkness resemble black Swallows or even bats as they cruise the waves feeding on plankton. These are much commoner than the Leach's Petrel, which is confined to the far north-west islands. Both are prized sightings. Adults remain deep ocean birds outside the breeding season.

ALL DUCK NOW in moult are said to be 'in eclipse'. They are all very vulnerable at this time. It is also the most difficult time to tell male from female.

ALMOST ALL SHELDUCK in Britain travel this month to special moulting places where they gather together for safety. Most go with other European birds to the Heligoland Bight. Others assemble in Bridgewater Bay and the Wash or Tay estuary. Birds that remain to guard the young ducklings of the year in the breeding waters are known as 'Aunties'.

RED-BREASTED MERGANSERS GATHER in August in bays and secluded rocky coastal areas of Wales and Scotland as they prepare to moult.

FLOCKS OF EIDER Duck leave their breeding grounds on the Farne Islands as well as coasts all around Scotland, and form tight packs out to sea where they moult.

Field and Farm

ONE OF THE big spectacular field events of the natural world in August is the marriage flight of the ants. All species of ant have their own air force consisting of high-flying males and queens. The queens will only mate with those males who can keep up with her. Birds know all about this grand occasion and gather in flocks to feast on the aerial congregation. Black-headed and Common Gulls are especially fond of the banquet, as are Starlings, Rooks and Jackdaws, House Martins and Swallows.

HOBBY FALCONS OFTEN nest on farmland with scattered clumps of trees, especially Scots pine. Their young fly for the first time in the middle of the month and will make a call very similar to that of a young Swift squealing in flight.

SPOTTED FLYCATCHERS, YELLOWHAMMERS, Goldfinches and Song Thrushes may all have second broods now.

YOU CAN TELL Pied Wagtail males from females by their white chins and throats. The female has a black chin and throat.

HARVEST TIME BRINGS many birds to the stubbles to glean spilt corn. Wood Pigeons digest the grain into a milky paste as they fly back to the woods to feed their squabs. Rooks enjoy the best time of the year for feeding and the local rookery may meet in hundreds. Mallard flight at dusk from lakes and ponds and feed all night on the grain.

MANY BIRDS DISAPPEAR from view now as they moult. Dunnocks especially creep into the bottom of bramble bushes or thick coppice and may not be seen again until late autumn. Blackbirds lose their crowns and look especially comical.

LOOSE FEATHERS LYING on the ground are a very useful guide to birds you may not have realised were around. For instance, those black feathers with large white dots belong to that secretive bird the Great Spotted Woodpecker.

WOOD PIGEONS CARRY hatched eggs away from their nests and drop them about 100 metres distant. These shells will show remains of fine red veins if they have hatched successfully, and will also be neatly in halves. Untidy breakage and/or signs of yellow yolk show that the eggs have been eaten by a predator, usually a Magpie, crow, Jay or squirrel.

YOUNG ROBINS APPEAR with their pale orange breasts. Pair bonding between adults breaks down now. Some females may stay and defend a territory against their former partners, but many migrate far to the south into France.

Moor and Mountain

SAWBILL DUCKS NOW come down the burns of the upland moors and mountains where they have been breeding. Red-breasted Mergansers have nested waterside in heather or marram clumps or down rabbit holes or in tree roots. Similar to Shelduck, 'Aunties' may guard up to 50 juveniles and so delay their own moults.

GOOSANDERS HAVE NESTED in the holes of pine trees across Scotland. In recent decades they have spread south into Wales and even the West Midlands. This may be due to less persecution by humans.

BOTH RED-BREASTED MERGANSERS and Goosanders feed on fish, which include trout and salmon. They grip slippery fish with the rough edges of their beaks. One of the old names for the Goosander was 'Jacksaw'.

AUGUST 12 HAS for a century and a half been the opening day for shooting Red Grouse. Shooters come from all over the world to hunt these birds. Nearly half a million birds exist today in the UK moorlands. The species, with careful management, has been known to reach densities of over 1,000 per square mile (650 per square kilometre) in Yorkshire. Management entails burning moors in regular strips to encourage fresh heather shoots, the principle food: and control of crows and foxes. But it is wet weather in July that is the major limiting factor, bringing about the death of many chicks.

Snow Buntings breeding on the Grampians and
north-west Highlands of Scotland often lose their first
brood due to May snowfall. Second broods as late
as July may suffer too but for a different reason: the
midsummer flush of insects on which the young are fed
for protein has passed its peak. Old birds suffer now
as well – they are moulting and lack of proper protein
during urgent feather replacement causes starvation.
Some birds solve this problem by scavenging for food
at roadside cafes or from mountain walkers.

Red-backed Shrikes are now virtually extinct
in Britain, but were common 150 years ago on
heathlands. One pair bred in the Shetlands in 1990.
This month birds from the continent pass down the
east coast.

Young White-tailed (Sea) Eagles will soon start to
disperse, and you might see them as far south as the
Norfolk coast later in the year. Once widely found
across the country and called Erne, the Sea Eagle was
described in the *Anglo-Saxon Chronicle* as usually
being present after battles, when:

> ... the grey coated eagle,
> white tailed, has his will of
> the corpses.

Sightings

1
....

2
....

3
....

4
....

5
....

6
....

7
....

8
....

9
....

10
....

11
....

12
....

13
....

14
....

August

15
....

16
....

17
....

18
....

19
....

20
....

21
....

22
....

23
....

24
....

25
....

26
....

27
....

28
....

29
....

30
....

31
....

September

Garden

ONE WAY TO have close-up views of birds in your garden is to allow ivy and creepers to grow on nearby trees or on the house itself. Spotted Flycatchers, Pied Wagtails and migrant birds will spend days feeding on the many different flies which like to hibernate in large masses in the dense cover. These harmless insects include drone flies, fruit flies, sawflies and lacewings.

GARDEN BIRD FEEDERS should now include proteins such as nuts and fat-balls as all birds now have to grow new feathers after the moult.

AUTUMN MIGRANTS SUCH as Chiffchaff and Willow Warbler, Blackcap and Garden Warbler, each need to lay down 5 grams of fat to fuel the journey to Africa. They can get this quickly from blackberries – so allow an area for them to grow if you can. The wilder your garden, the more variety of insects and so birds will appear. An over-groomed garden is a barren desert for birds.

ROBINS FEEDING ON the worms you disturb as you dig evolved this behaviour thousands of years ago around mammals such as deer, cattle, horses, moles and in more recent times, rabbits. In more northern Scandinavian countries a close relative, the Bluethroat, befriends gardeners in the same way.

September

MALE AND FEMALE Robins now form separate territories, each about half the size held by the pair in summer months.

VERY OCCASIONALLY A Hoopoe appears on garden lawns in early autumn in the south-east. Lawns can provide the food they need: crane flies, grasshoppers, moths, ants, earwigs, spiders, worms, centipedes and woodlice. You will never forget this bizarre bird if you ever see one. The long thin down-curved beak, enormous crest, pinkish plumage and flashing black and white wings give it the appearance of a clown among birds. It breeds south and east of Britain and winters in Africa.

BULLFINCHES MAY MATE for life. Unlike most garden birds, they do not split up after breeding into same sex flocks. Whenever you see the bright pink chest and black cap and beak of this chubby finch you can be almost sure that hovering somewhere nearby is the pale beige female, also searching for weed seeds such as buttercup, herb bennet, dock, wood sage and clematis.

BLACKCAP WARBLERS LINGER much later than other warblers, except perhaps Chiffchaffs. Main movements out of the country will be during the first two weeks of September with 200-plus birds in one day at Beachy Head in Sussex.

Woodland

FROM THE SCOTTISH valley woods, Willow Warblers, Chiffchaffs, Wood Warblers and other small migrants pass south in a steady stream through the Esk valley marshes on the southern shores of the Solway. A well-known place to see them is at Grune Point, west of Carlisle, and in the Calvo and Skinburness Marshes. Many then assemble on the south coast of England, especially Devil's Dyke near Brighton or Church Norton at Pagham Harbour. Official birders spend hours counting these migrations: the sight is enjoyable for its own sake.

COCK WREN NESTS made as invitation presents to females now start to come in useful for another reason – communal roosts for the family and neighbours. They are constructed of moss wound with dead leaves and grass into round hollow balls the size of an orange with a small side entrance. They are not lined with feathers: the female will only do that if she intends to lay eggs there.

THERE ARE ONLY 3,000 pairs of Hawfinches currently present in England and Wales – much of their old woodland habitat was destroyed in the 1987 hurricane. This secretive bird thrives especially where wild cherry and hawthorn grow as the pips can be opened by their strong large beaks. In September family parties have daily forays out to special seed trees and the birds return to dense woodland in late afternoon to roost. They make a *'tick'* call as they fly.

September

JAYS AS WELL as squirrels hide hazelnuts (with plump kernels only) in the leaf litter or grass verges of woods – they know exactly where these places are and will dig them out as the winter progresses. Continental Jays come into the east coast to overwinter in England. Up to a hundred can occasionally be seen feeding on acorns from hedgerow trees in East Anglia. Their small striped blue and black wing feathers dropped during the late summer moult were once highly prized as decoration in men's hat bands.

ROOSTS OF CORMORANTS may assemble in riverside woodlands. Some birds have used cathedrals as roosts if within reach of water, for example at Chichester, West Sussex, only a few miles from the harbour.

YEW WOODS ON the South and North Downs will from now on through the winter during daylight have the gentle tapping sounds of Great Tits opening yew tree fruit pips. They find those by the thousand lying under female trees and take them one by one up into the branches.

Wetland and Coastal

ARCTIC TERNS PASS our coasts on their pole-to-pole migration. Some may have nested within 700 miles of the North Pole and may get as far south as the Antarctic continent in December before starting their journey back again. This is the longest journey of any bird in the world.

ALL FOUR SKUA species – Arctic, Great, Long-tailed, and Pomarine – start their migrations south; one good place to see them this month would be the Firth of Forth near Grangemouth. Skuas are like large, brown Gulls but with longer central tail feathers. They are hawk-like and will kill smaller seabirds or chase them to make them disgorge their crops of food. A Great Skua has been known to force down a Whooper Swan and kill it, and also to kill sickly lambs.

BIRDWATCHERS TREASURE SIGHTINGS of Curlew Sandpipers and Little Stints, two of the small waders now on passage south. They can be found singly or in very small groups all down the east coast at such wetlands as Cresswell Ponds in Northumberland, Scolt Head in Norfolk and Sidlesham Pool in Sussex. As they will often be in the company of the Common Dunlin, identification pictures are essential.

THE RIVER CATCHMENTS of the Humber estuary contain Fairburn Ings on the river Aire just north of Pontefract. This wetland is a catchment for gatherings of Swallows and Sand Martins roosting in reed beds. Many southern reed beds will also contain, for a brief while, large numbers of these birds.

WIGEON ARRIVE ON estuaries and inland lakes which have grassland surrounds on which they graze. Many adults will still be coming out of moult (eclipse), so be aware that the drakes that normally show large white wing patches may still have brown feathers instead. The moult may not be totally complete until November.

THE AVON, WELLAND and Trent valleys of the Midlands have many gravel pit lakes, sewage farms and reservoirs where returning waders and wild duck drop in for short or long stays now. Green, Wood and Common Sandpiper, Snipe, Redshank, and occasional Greenshank, together with Teal, will make an exciting day's viewing.

BITTERNS FROM HOLLAND begin westerly movement to reed beds in England. Sometimes only half a hectare of reeds surrounding a pond or a riverbank will hold one of these birds that look like huge brown moths as they fly. More specialised, Bluethroats and Barred Warblers may arrive on east coast saltings.

Field and Farm

STARLINGS GATHER INTO vast flocks called 'murmurations' for the winter – one of the largest roosts is in the Somerset Levels RSPB reserve reed beds. The birds make rapidly changing patterns like holograms. Others gather into warm safe city buildings such as those around Brighton Marina. Even smallish flocks provide marvellous entertainment.

WRYNECKS PASS SOUTH through England to Africa from their breeding places in Norway and Sweden, possibly Scotland, in August and September. These small brown and grey Woodpeckers look rather like Nightjars and have a call like that of a falcon. Once common in Britain they are now mostly migrant visitors. They have a liking for cottage lawns surrounded by trees, where they hunt for ants for a day or two before continuing south. Their name comes from the ability to twist their necks (owl-like) right round. Wryneck intrigued our forebears with their calls, their nest behaviour when disturbed and their appearance, giving rise to names such as Hisser, Peel-bird and Snake-bird.

EARLY AUTUMN, WITH its warmth and food gleaned in harvest fields, makes Rooks liable to play out of sheer joy in living. This *joie de vivre* can be seen in the fields when birds floating high up on thermals suddenly take to skydiving. They return to earth with daredevil corkscrewing dives known as 'whiffling'. Wild geese will also indulge.

HOUSE MARTINS GATHER in the south before migrating, usually at the end of the month. By day they may hunt for insects above wooded valleys in the South Downs. They often choose the same warm roof of a farm building to roost by night or rest on by day, year after year.

HOBBY FALCONS WILL follow the Swallow and Martin flocks south, feeding on them all the way down into Africa. They also feed on dragonflies and butterflies along the South Downs.

LOCAL DEWPONDS IN otherwise dry farmland valleys are wonderful places to see migrants this month. Typical daily counts on one small Sussex pond include 800 House Martins, ten Redstarts, five Nightingales, two Whinchats, ten Blackcap Warblers, as well as 30 resident species coming in to drink.

MIGRANTS SUCH AS Wheatear, Whinchat and Stonechat returning south will often use the same wire fences to perch on as they did in spring on their way north. If you get to know your local farmland well and keep records over the years, March and September are good months to collect information for your annual county bird reports.

Moor and Mountain

LIKE HUMANS, SUMMER bird visitors now
leave the mountains as weather deteriorates
but the hardy residents – Grouse,
Corvids, Eagles – remain.

SOME DOTTEREL THAT bred in Scotland are now
already down in the Persian Gulf and Red Sea shores.
Others may linger on the east coast, on shore or farm
fields into November, and there is the occasional over-
winterer in Norfolk or Kent.

GOLDEN PLOVER IN moult after breeding lose
their handsome black throats and chests that have
contrasted so visibly with the gold and white of their
backs. They track southwards, sometimes in large
flocks, to lowland fields and to estuaries on the east
and south coasts: some travel south as far as Morocco.
They often consort with flocks of Lapwings but are
usually just slightly separated and in the sky make
quite different patterns.

GREENSHANK ARE ONE of the most elegant and
superbly refined shapes of all waders, and Scotland
plays host to 1 per cent of the world population with
about 1,000 pairs breeding in the north-west
Highlands – this is the highest number in
the European Community.

But damage to their breeding habitat from drainage of mountain mires where the chicks need to feed on insect protein, increasing access by all-terrain vehicles to quiet breeding areas, and the modern curse of planting evergreen tree crops, is rapidly spoiling the chances of this bird's survival. Some now migrate to the tropics, with Siberian breeders even reaching Australia, but some spend mild winters here in the south.

PTARMIGAN GRADUALLY CHANGE their plumage as the summer moves into autumn. You might be able to see this remarkable moult much more easily at ski-lift stations where the birds, together with Red Grouse, have become fairly tame in recent years. In summer the male is in heather-mix brown and grey with white flecks and patches. Autumn sees the plumage alter to more of a dove grey on the back mottled with white, though the crown and centre back stripe still continue with heathery tints. The breast has become pale grey with much more white on the flanks. Most birds remain above 2,500 feet (800 metres) and up to 4,000 feet (1,300 metres) while the autumn weather remains fine.

THE GOLDEN EAGLE has moulted gradually which (unlike duck and geese) allows it to remain airborne. Its primary wing feathers, a foot in length, each working like separate propellers at the tips of the wings, may occasionally be found.

Sightings

1
....

2
....

3
....

4
....

5
....

6
....

7
....

8
....

9
....

10
....

11
....

12
....

13
....

14
....

15
....

16
....

17
....

18
....

19
....

20
....

21
....

22
....

23
....

24
....

25
....

26
....

27
....

28
....

29
....

30
....

October

Garden

Now is the time to overhaul nest boxes and/or install new ones. This gives the birds time to get used to them before the spring. They should be positioned in the shade. The RSPB sell a full range for many species including those for Swift, Kestrel and Spotted Fly-catcher, as well as the usual garden birds.

During the winter you may find some nest boxes get taken over by dormice if you live next to old hazel coppice woodland; some become the homes of wood mice, yellow-necked mice or even weasels.

If you have Great Spotted Woodpeckers visiting the bird table, you can easily tell the sexes apart. Males have red on the back of their heads – female heads are just black and white. Juveniles have a large full red crown. Juvenile Green Woodpeckers have heavily barred throats and underparts, making them appear grey. Their red crowns are developing well but are not as obvious as those of the parents.

A HERON CAN see the gleam of water from a quarter of a mile away so it may spot your pond with its stock of pet fish as it flies over. To prevent them eating all, put a net across a foot or more above the surface with a tripwire round the pond edge. Garden centres (and gun dealers) usually sell decoy Herons, which tell live intruders the pond is already occupied!

OUT OF 100 Robins' eggs laid in spring and summer, 42 juveniles normally survive till now. By this time next year ten will be alive. Another year on, three, then two, and then only one will reach the age of five. Cats, unfortunately, are one of the biggest predators.

GOLDFINCHES WILL VISIT your garden for Niger seed, but a cheaper alternative is to have a few plants of the thistle family in your garden. These so-called weeds are one of the best nectar sources for bees, then the plants provide food for finches in the autumn. Spear and scotch thistles are less invasive and more attractive than creeping thistles. They are easily controlled, being biennials with a single large leaf rosette in the year before flowering.

AS THE NIGHTS grow colder, birds have to preserve enough heat to keep alive. Pigeons hunch up to reduce surface area, raising feathers to trap warm air. Tits, Crows and Starlings creep close to share body heat. Woodpeckers roost inside old nest holes. Blackbirds, Sparrows and Thrushes roost under ivy canopies.

Woodland

TAWNY OWLS BEGIN calling again, setting the boundaries of next spring's territories. The males hoot half an hour after sunset and again at intervals throughout the night until half an hour before dawn. The male calls *'Who?'* and the female answers *'You twit!'* – which in her language means 'Come and get me then'.

LARGE FLOCKS OF Wood Pigeons arrive on the east coast, numbering several thousand birds. These may have come from Scotland and northern England or from the continent and Scandinavia. They prospect the oak woods of Essex first for the acorn crop; one bird swallowing about 20 acorns per day.

WOODCOCK ARRIVE ON the east coast from breeding grounds as far away as the middle of Siberia. They usually make this 2,000–3,000-mile migration very quickly, in a few days if the wind is easterly during the high pressure that usually develops on autumn full moons. The birds are often so exhausted when they arrive they have been known in the past sometimes to fall into the streets and gardens of Norfolk villages in hundreds, but they move on west at daylight. Thus the term 'a fall of Woodcock', as the group noun is explained.

PHEASANT SHOOTING STARTS on 1 October. The breeds today are hybrids of six true species brought into this country by wealthy travellers as early as Norman times and through to the Victorian era. Although the characteristics are now muddled up you can still pick out plumage differences in cock birds that relate back centuries. For instance, white neck-rings belonged to the Mongolian races, or Chinese ring-neck. Plain green-necked birds were Southern Caucasians; purple necks with green flanks were Southern Green from Japan; Prince of Wales with white wing patches. Hybrids today may be pure black birds.

NUTCRACKERS SOMETIMES FLY west in autumn to this country if the weather in Siberia is particularly harsh or the acorn crop fails there. These birds are rather like Jays except their plumage is brown flecked with white. They belong in the crow family. They call *'krarr'* five or six times in rapid succession.

ONE WAY TO help ensure Wrens survive frosts and predators is, instead of burning or tidying away brash, to leave stacks of it (cut small branches) into which they can hide and keep warm. Ivy tods and brambles also provide shelter. They need a good supply of spiders and other insects to feed on.

Wetland and Coastal

THIS IS THE peak month of the year in Britain for numbers of Pink-footed Geese, with over 300,000 arriving from Iceland. There are 50 main wintering wetlands. The RSPB reserve at Loch of Strathbeg, Aberdeenshire, has up to 60,000 birds, the biggest single flock.

THE NORTH NORFOLK coast with three main sites has over 100,000 Pink-footed Geese, which feed off the tops from sugar-beet left after harvesting. The spectacle of these birds in flight across sunset or sunrise is one to be treasured.

THE REPTILIAN-LOOKING CORMORANT is ubiquitous, hanging out its wings in a black cross to dry. Be aware that the smaller Shag is very similar.

TWO RACES OF White-fronted Goose now arrive in the UK for the winter. Fifteen hundred European or Russian geese visit southern England river meadows from the Severn Estuary at Slimbridge WWT to the Avon meadows near Salisbury and east to the Swale in Kent. Numbers are in decline here but have increased to almost a million in the Netherlands. They breed on Russian tundra. The pink beak is the diagnostic feature.

THIRTEEN THOUSAND GREENLAND White-fronts winter on Islay in West Scotland and the Wexford Slobs in Ireland, having bred in Greenland. This is the total world population. For Greenlands, the orange-yellow beak is the diagnostic feature.

SHELDUCK DRIFT BACK to the estuaries from their moulting grounds in Heligoland and Bridgewater Bay. Many of 'our' birds now winter in the Netherlands instead, so we now have only 50,000, mainly in Mersey, Dee, Morecambe Bay, Wash, Humber and Severn estuaries.

ONE OF THE most extraordinary of all our ducks is the Mandarin from East Asia, which has continued to increase after introduction before 1745. The 600 birds counted each year are probably a fraction of what is in the UK – the estimate is 7,000. Woodland lakes and river valleys surrounded by dense trees are its habitat, and more study to find them all is needed.

RUBBISH TIPS IN London's catchment are places to sort out Gulls – 16,000 feed at one tip alone. About 14 different species totalling 300,000 birds could be seen in Britain in winter. Sorting them all out is testing for any birder.

SANDWICH, COMMON AND Arctic Tern can still be seen this month on south-and east-coast harbours as the late birds start their 6,000-mile journeys south.

BRENT GEESE NOW start to arrive at south-coast harbours.

Field and Farm

LARGE FLOCKS OF Fieldfares appear on the East Anglian coast in mid October, having crossed from Sweden overnight. They usually fly west at treetop height, stopping to eat hawthorn and yew berries en route. The very first birds will have been seen in August. They remain in these flocks throughout the winter as they are used to living in colonies in the forests where they breed. Being together has many advantages for both nesting and overwintering. Mainly, if the nest site is threatened by a predator such as a hawk or fox, there is a cunning plan to drive it away: the birds dive on the enemy and release the contents of their bowels on its head.

HEN HARRIERS RETURN from the moors to spend the winter on upland fields and downs mainly in this month but can be as early as August. Their favourite hunting grounds used to be stubble fields where flocks of Finches gathered to feed on weed seeds and spilt grain. Nowadays harvest fields are ploughed almost immediately, so that habitat has been lost to them. They may now find these feeding flocks around pheasant holding-strips of millet and sunflowers.

TREE SPARROWS ARE much rarer than House Sparrows but very small flocks might be located on fields. Look for the chestnut crown of the male and the shriller chirrup.

October

SKYLARKS START TO arrive from breeding grounds across the continent and steppes of Russia, especially when high-pressure weather systems develop easterly winds with early cold weather. They search wide-open fields and downs, uplands and heaths for seeds of charlock, chickweed, sorrel, sow thistle and the minute fauna of wild places including spiders, caterpillars, beetle larvae, and small earthworms.

MOST SWALLOWS WILL have departed by now but on the south coast flocks of 200 may still be seen, ready to depart at any moment, although stragglers remain into November.

ONE TRICK THAT birds have to get rid of parasites such as mites and flies is to sit in a nest of wood or red ants. These insects swarm over the plumage and squirt formic acid into the feathers. Apparently about one third of the pests are killed off in this way. Blackbirds, Pipits and Corvids are particularly known to do this. Pheasants will dust in hot ash from old bonfires. A Jay is known to have placed a burning cigarette end under its wing for the same effect!

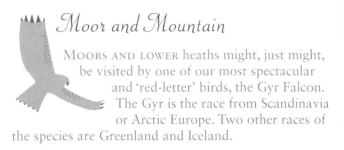

Moor and Mountain

MOORS AND LOWER heaths might, just might, be visited by one of our most spectacular and 'red-letter' birds, the Gyr Falcon. The Gyr is the race from Scandinavia or Arctic Europe. Two other races of the species are Greenland and Iceland.

THE GREENLAND FALCON that my father, Henry Williamson, mentions in Chapter 9 of *Tarka the Otter* was sadly caught by a rabbit trapper on Braunton Burrows in north Devon in the mid 1920s. The bird was stuffed and today resides in a glass case in Braunton Museum.

THE 420 PAIRS of Golden Eagles in Britain are part of the 5,000 pairs in Europe west of the Ural Mountains in Russia: all divided into five ecological groups. Under 2,000 of these are part of the montane group found in Britain and Scandinavia. The British birds therefore represent roughly 7 per cent of the total European population: a fine success story.

BUZZARDS ARE LIMITED in mountainous areas by scarcity of tree and crag nest sites, and food is often difficult to find. This makes the small farm fields of the lower slopes important: hedgerows and field banks hold voles and possibly rats; sheep grazing encourages earthworms. These are all important factors if the Buzzard is to live out the winter.

OVER 100 PAIRS of Ospreys that bred in the Highland lochs are now en route to Africa. Most stop off on south-coast estuaries and lakes in early autumn, allowing southerners the chance to admire this magnificent bird. As they fly overhead they are instantly recognisable by their white underparts and kinked leading edge to their wings at the carpal (wrist) joint. Be sure to check that it is not a Rough-legged Buzzard, Honey Buzzard, or if you're abroad in the south, the three eagles that are also white beneath: Bonnelli's, Booted and Short-toed.

MOORLAND CLIFFS OF the west coasts are now the playgrounds of that curious crow, the Chough. These birds are somehow far more attractive to us than any others of the family with their slim, curved crimson beaks and legs. They are now to be seen off-duty after the breeding season, playing with great skill in the windy updraughts. This is one of the most aerobatic of all birds as they hover, soar, tumble and fly upside down.

SEVERE WINTERS SUCH as that of 1947 can cut the Crested Tit population in Speyside woodlands by 70 per cent. This geographically isolated Scottish sub-species *(Parus cristatus scoticus)* thrives best in Scots pine woods.

Sightings

1

2

3

4

5

6

7

8

9

10

11

12

13

14

October

15
....

16
....

17
....

18
....

19
....

20
....

21
....

22
....

23
....

24
....

25
....

26
....

27
....

28
....

29
....

30
....

31
....

November

Garden

MOST OF THE young birds you carefully helped to nurture during the summer will suddenly disappear as they feel the urge to find their own new world over the horizon.

MALE STARLINGS START to explore old nesting holes as November's full-moon fine weather brings back a memory of spring. The females respond with a most curious display of running back and forth along the bare branches of the trees or rooftops to attract attention.

ABOUT HALF OF the female Robin population flies south to France for the winter, the rest remains here – but they then have to defend their territories against the males.

NUTHATCHES CAN CLIMB upwards or downwards on trees without using their tails as a prop, unlike woodpeckers. Treecreepers tend to start at the bottom of a tree and work upwards looking like clockwork mice, but also hang upside down under branches. They are nowhere near so obvious as the Nuthatch.

November

MANY LARGE GARDENS are suitable for the Green Woodpecker: they need a lawn and one or two dead tree trunks, typically beech or ash, in the shrubbery. They will feed on ants and beetle larvae and feel secure in the cover. Males can only be distinguished from females by their red moustaches.

TIT FAMILIES NOW band into larger groups, which help them to explore nearby woods. Young Blackbirds often join continental migrants travelling south-west, as will Robins. Just like humans, some youngsters try to remain with their parents but are usually chased off. If they remain local, then they have to learn to keep out of the way.

NOW IS THE time to think about planting berry shrubs in the garden to attract birds in the future. Hawthorn is one of the best – its cream-pink-white blossom, so lovely for us to see and smell, also attracts insects such as bees and butterflies and many different species of fly that are the food of Warbler and Finch nestlings. The autumn berry crop is of enormous value to resident and migrant Thrushes.

OTHER BERRY SPECIES to be enjoyed are cotoneaster, japonica and stranvaesia. Sunflowers left to seed are not only attractive but a very useful source of food. Michaelmas daisies are another useful source. The seeds of clematis ('old man's beard') and buddleia are eaten by tits and Bullfinches. They will also eat most 'weed' seeds such as dock, sage, herb bennet and plantains. There is a great deal to be said for having a wild garden.

Woodland

RAVENS WILL ALREADY have begun, however briefly, their courtship displays. They roll over in mid-air and loop the loop especially during that period when the weather is warm and still during a waxing moon.

THIS TIME WAS known as 'Goose Summer', when our ancestors gorged on geese at the feast of St Martin. That name was then shortened to 'gossamer', a name for the mass of spider silk spun on meadows looking like sheets of silver in clear moonlight, and in the sun's slanting rays.

HOPEFULLY, MOST OF the two million pairs of Willow Warblers which arrived here in April will now be back with their young in their winter quarters south of the Sahara in the Sudan: Mali, Niger, Nigeria, Chad.

THE 200,000 PAIRS of Redstarts will also have arrived in the Sudan in Guinea, Upper Volta, Ivory Coast and other African states.

SPARROWHAWKS ARE BEAUTIFUL but dangerous. They will fly low along a hedgerow and make a sudden lunge into a cluster of Finches or Tits, or onto the bird table. The slightly smaller male has a slate-grey back with chestnut barring underparts.

OF THE 80,000 Goshawks in Europe, about 600 live
in Britain and are increasing. They require large areas
of forest and are skilful in avoiding humans. They
are like a large version of a Sparrowhawk – they slip
through tree trunks silently and swiftly, surprising
birds and mammals. Circles of Pigeon feathers on the
ground provide evidence that they are present. This
clue, however, could also show that a Sparrowhawk
is hunting the woods. Often the only way to see a
Goshawk is to keep those eyes on the skies: in winter
and spring Goshawks soar high in courtship flights
when you can see their size – and note the conspicuous
white under-tail coverts.

MISTLE THRUSHES FEED on yew berries grown on the
female trees. Yew berries are like tiny red lanterns.
They are relict fir cones and contain a sweet sticky
juice, which is edible, but the inner pip is deadly
poisonous. Birds pass these pips straight through,
helping regeneration.

WOOD DUCK, INTRODUCED in 1870 and wild in very
small numbers (probably under 50) in England, have
come back to full plumage in November. They are also
called Summer Duck, and Carolina Duck,
following their American names. Their
bizarre green, white, yellow and purple
face and body patterns are most singular.
They nest in small numbers in trees in
southern England and are very shy.

Wetland and Coastal

FULMAR NOW RETURN to breeding cliffs around the coast if the weather is calm – but when the fierce wind blows they will fly back to the open ocean. Their early breeding display this month is very noisy as the pairs remember old bonds, consider new, repel hopefuls: all with a guttural cacophony of noise and argument.

AVOCETS HAVE NOT entirely deserted their breeding grounds which are mainly on the east coast from the Wash to the Isle of Sheppey. Many fly south to winter in the south and south-west estuaries and on down to France. Harbours on the south coast – Chichester, Poole, Exe, etc. – all have small numbers during the winter months. They are the most elegant and unmistakeable of waders, with long, thin upturned beaks and black and white plumage.

BLACK-TAILED GODWITS ARE now here from their breeding grounds in the Baltic and continental marshes. They spend the winter on mudflats and flooded meadows, somewhat similar to their breeding areas.

BAR-TAILED GODWITS, HAVING bred in Lapland, seem to require a slightly different wintering habitat: more wide-open sandy estuaries. The two species are very alike – but you can tell them apart easily as they fly away. Bar-tails have a white rump with thin black bars on the tail, whereas Black-tails have a white rump with a single black end.

PERHAPS THE MOST elegant duck is the Pintail. The cock has a chocolate-coloured head with a cream stripe up the side. Its flanks are lined with very fine grey stripes over white, which give the appearance of ruffled water. Its very long tail gave it the name of 'sea pheasant' in times past. The female is mottled, dead-leaf brown and can be identified from Gadwall and Mallard Ducks by its longer neck. Look for Pintails especially at clean sewage outfalls in estuaries or where mudflats are especially soft.

ANOTHER VERY STRIKING male duck is the Smew. It is pure white with thin jet-black markings down its neck and flanks. These ducks are found on London reservoirs and gravel-pit lakes in winter. In frosty weather they will dive under the ice to catch tiny fish with their beaks – serrated like fret-saw blades.

CHARCOAL PLUMAGED, WHITE-FACED and fond of town ponds and shallow lakes, the Coot is familiar all year round but especially so from November when continental breeders fly in to spend a milder winter here.

Field and Farm

FIELDFARES OCCASIONALLY continue to sing even in winter, but more especially on warm and fine days. Their song is described as a 'feeble warble interrupted by wheezes and chuckles'. When in a flock, the sound is like chabbling water.

REDWING WILL SOMETIMES feed on winkles on the tide edge near farmland. These snails are especially easy to find when the water drops just after high tide at dusk.

SONG THRUSHES HAVE preferred diets over the year. Earthworms are their favourite food in spring, pupating caterpillars in summer and snails in autumn and winter – but they are almost the only readily available food then. There are over a million pairs in Britain.

CETTI'S WARBLER IS not just a purely wetland bird but may be found in dense bramble and willow scrub in damp farmland or along canals and slow streams in southern England and Wales. They may be resident all winter. The song is sudden, loud and explosive, but you will not necessarily see the bird, as this small brown Warbler skulks unseen in thick cover. It was not known in this country until 1970, having moved north from Spain and France.

LITTLE EGRETS MAY now be seen in farmland along brooks and streams well inland in the south, and spreading rapidly outwards. Their pure white crest plumes were once in such demand as a fashion accessory from birds shot in Egypt that this small heron became rare. Individual birds will stake a claim to one small stretch of water year after year and can become quite tame by footpaths.

CROW WOOD, ALSO called Cra Wid, in Aberdeenshire has been winter roost to up to 65,000 Rooks in years past. The wood is at Hatton Castle, south of Turriff. This is the largest roost in Europe. Other large spectacular roosts are in Norfolk, Suffolk, Essex and Wiltshire. The birds are drawn from several square miles of agricultural land and arrive in a noisy mass. There may be one and a half million Rooks in Britain.

IN THE SEVERE winter of 1963, Snipe and Woodcock came into cattle yards for warmth and worms – the only way they could survive without migrating to Spain.

GREY WAGTAILS FOLLOW streams through fields, villages and even towns and cities as they migrate south as far as Spain during the early winter. This grey, yellow, black and white, elegant bird of tumbling streams suffers badly in hard weather.

Moor and Mountain

SNIPE ARE MAINLY a moorland breeding bird. Their lowland breeding marshes have been heavily trampled by cattle except at a few lowland nature reserves but moorland bogs and rough pastures on mountain valley terrain are still reasonably safe for the 30,000 pairs breeding in Britain. Many of these descend into lower marshes and coastal saltings for the winter.

MISTLE THRUSHES BREED as far north as the Orkneys but their very high numbers between 1800 and 1960 are now declining. A dominant male will defend a fruit berry tree such as rowan, yew or hawthorn with great pugnacity, seeing off flocks of Fieldfares, other Thrushes and Pigeons. Such a bird will be more successful the following spring and may have more than one mate as a result. Apart from that belligerent display you may find the bird difficult to find in winter, unless it gives a sudden brief burst of song. It will also feed on meadows and ploughed fields.

PINE FORESTS NOW growing on lowland heaths are where you will find the wandering flocks of Siskins, Redpolls and Crossbills in winter. Siskins have spread rapidly in Britain because the 1950s forest evergreen plantings have matured, providing habitat. The population grew from 30,000 to 300,000 in just 20 years as a result.

ONE OF THE best ways to see Siskins, which are pretty, lemony-yellow striped birds, close enough for easy identification is to find a stream, pond, or mire close enough to the woods where these birds will come fluttering down like fairies to drink in dry weather. Their diet of dry tree seeds makes them very thirsty.

THE REDPOLL'S RATTLING flight call should attract your attention to the skies. Mainly this will be above birch woods where they are feeding. Birch often follows clear felling on marginal land such as moors and heaths. Males have pink breasts and red 'polls'. Mealy Redpoll are paler; Arctic Redpoll paler still, more greyish white.

CROSSBILLS ARE BIGGER, almost brick-red (female yellowish-grey), unmistakeably cross-billed and fork-tailed, and tend to stay where fir species provide cones for them to pull open and eat seeds, dropping cones to the ground.

THE LINNET'S WINTER range is very similar to its breeding range – north to the Orkneys. The bird is attracted especially to gorse habitats and is found on most uplands, but absent from mountains. The seed food is fat-hen, charlock, penny-cress, scurvy grass, shepherd's purse, wild cabbage and oilseed rape.

Sightings

1
....

2
....

3
....

4
....

5
....

6
....

7
....

8
....

9
....

10
....

11
....

12
....

13
....

14
....

15

16

17

18

19

20

21

22

23

24

25

26

27

28

29

30

December

Garden

SONG THRUSHES HAVE already begun territory claims last month and will sing vividly this month in mild weather. Listen for their song repetitions. The opening phrase is often repeated three times. I am always reminded of Mozart's opening to his 40th symphony when I hear the beginning of its song. Could the composer have copied that song? The poet Robert Browning famously noted in 'Home-Thoughts, from Abroad':

> That's the wise thrush,
> He sings each song twice over,
> Lest you should think
> He never could recapture
> That first fine careless rapture.

GREAT TITS SHOW their rank with the black stripe that runs down throat and chest and belly. The bigger this is, the more senior the bird. Usually the very sight of the chest is enough to send a rival off. If not, the bird will point its beak, crouch, and half open its wings to make itself look bigger. Squabbling at the bird table is rife, especially as the birds start to come into breeding form. Old names for the Great Tit include Oxeye, Pickcheese, Tomtit, Tom Collier and Sit-ye-down.

IN TOWN AND village gardens near the sea, Black-headed Gulls often come down to bird tables in winter. They will grab large items and take them off, when all the others will give noisy chase. Town and city gardens are more likely to have Herring Gulls, which often nest on the roofs in spring, again with much noisy calling. These bigger gulls are bold enough to attempt to take the chicks of Peregrine Falcons nesting on tall buildings.

BLACKCAP WARBLERS ON bird tables (in the south) now, breed mainly in central Europe, not Britain. Our breeders tend to be normal spring migrants.

ONE HUNDRED DIFFERENT weed and tree seed species are known to be part of the diet of Chaffinches.

GREENFINCHES ARE EASILY attracted to bird tables but seed dispersers and water containers must be kept scrupulously clean as they are particularly prone to the disease trichomonosis. Their numbers have been decimated in recent years.

PROVISION OF DRINKING water attracts birds to your garden but, ideally, must be changed every day.

SEVERAL THOUSAND RING-NECKED Parakeets now live wild very successfully in southern Britain. Brought here as captive birds, their proper home is in more exotic Africa and Asia. They compete with native hole-nesters such as Woodpeckers and Nuthatches. They can lay eggs in January in mild winters.

Woodland

HUNTING THE WREN was a common pastime for 26 December – St Stephen's Day – in Europe for many centuries, and had its origins in symbolic winter solstice sacrifice that goes back to prehistoric times. This bizarre ritual involved chasing and killing a Wren and carrying it home ceremoniously. The Wren was thought to be 'king of the birds' and its slayer would adopt that title. Later, it was thought that killing a Wren on Boxing Day would bring good luck for the year.

THE CUSTOM HAD many names: 'Jenty' in Derbyshire, 'Shacking' in Warwickshire, 'Wrenning Day' in Cumberland, 'Toodling' in Buckinghamshire and 'Deckan o' tha Wren' in Scotland. The custom finally ended in Northern Ireland in the 1950s.

FIRECRESTS CAN BE identified from Goldcrests by their black eye-stripe and white supercilium stripe above. Also, Firecrest crowns are a stronger orange and their shoulders are darker greeny-gold. The Goldcrest's eye is enhanced by pale grey eye shadow. Both birds suffer badly in cold weather but numbers bounce back as the hens can lay up to ten eggs twice in the season – more usually six or seven. Both have benefitted from Forestry Commission fir plantations in the last 60 years.

GOLDCRESTS WERE ONCE called 'Woodcock Pilots' because they arrived on the east coast from Russia a few days before the Woodcock.

LISTEN OUT ON calm moonlit nights for the love call of Tawny Owls – a long bubbling note, quite magical to hear.

LONG-TAILED TITS BAND together in winter in small flocks but may die in severe winter weather as they chiefly depend on tiny insects and larvae found along branches. To keep warm they huddle together into a tight ball of a dozen birds.

WILLOW TITS ARE very similar to Marsh Tits but the Willow is paler than the Marsh, with a greyish back, matt black crown and a larger black throat patch, and a barred marking on the closed wing. The Marsh Tit has an even, brownish back and a more prominent black crown but a smaller throat patch. In the breeding season the Willow Tit's call note, a melancholy '*chay*', is diagnostic against the Marsh Tit's more explosive '*pit-choo*'. The Willow Tit excavates its own nest hole while the Marsh uses a ready-made hollow in a tree.

Wetland and Coastal

A SMALL COLONY of Common Cranes returned to the Norfolk Broads to breed in 1979 and nowadays there are up to 40 in winter around Horsey Mere. Its eggs were protected under Henry VIII in 1544, but it became extinct in the eighteenth century. It resembles a large Grey Heron but has a black neck. The tail is also black and droops with long loose feathers.

ONE OF THE most noticeable birds of the salt marsh is the Redshank. There are about 60,000 in Britain. At high tide all around our coasts they gather into 'trips' to roost on the same stretch of salting for decade after decade. When feeding they space themselves out across upper shore mudflats and guard each area from neighbours. Here you can easily see their orange-red legs and beaks.

SPOTTED REDSHANK (150 in Britain) are pale and dark grey with longer beaks. Redshank call a rapid 'tu tu tu'. Greenshank have a similar call but slower. Spotted Redshank call 'tchuit'.

DEEP-SEA DUCK HAVE recently become very rare in Britain. About 2,000 Scaup dive for shellfish in bays and estuaries. They resemble a slightly enlarged Tufted Duck, the male of both species having broad white flanks and black necks and heads.

ABOUT 4,000 SCOTERS form small 'rafts' offshore. The males are dark brown (seeming black in most light conditions). There are six hundred Velvet Scoters which have a white eye-patch and a distinct white speculum (secondary flight feathers) seen when flying.

EIGHT THOUSAND PAIRS of Ringed Plovers breed inland and around the coast. In winter half this number can be seen on the coast, mainly the Humber, Ribble, North Norfolk, Wash, Solway and Morecambe Bay. Nests are very vulnerable as the eggs are not visible on shingle beaches and get stepped on and destroyed. Foxes, dogs, and other predators also decimate.

TWELVE THOUSAND SHOVELER Ducks are counted each winter by the Wetland Bird Survey (WEBS) across Britain. Best viewing places are on the Ouse Washes, Somerset Levels, Rutland Water and Breydon Water.

IDENTIFYING THE FOUR different species of Diver in winter on coasts and lochs can be quite a challenge: 1,000 Red-throated, 100 Black-throated, 300 Great Northern, one White-billed – all in winter plumage – can be found scattered across the country.

SIMILARLY, THE WINTER-PLUMAGED Grebes are often difficult to find and identify. WEBS-count totals average 5,000 Little, 8,000 Great Crested, eight Red-necked, 90 Black-necked, 150 Slavonian.

Field and Farm

COLLARED DOVES IN winter collect in small flocks around grain stores and cattle yards as an easy food source, just as they do in India and the Middle East.

ESTIMATED NUMBERS OF Wood Pigeons in Britain are currently five million. Fifty years ago the food was clover, buttercup leaves and chickweed. Now they feed on oilseed rape throughout the winter but still attack new-sown grain. Acorns and beech mast give protein to replace feathers in autumn.

IVY LEFT ON trees provides berries to feed Blackbirds as well as Pigeons, lasting through the winter into spring.

IN 2004 SOME young Great Bustards from Russia were successfully reintroduced onto Salisbury Plain. The bird had become extinct in Britain by the mid 1830s despite having its eggs protected (the first ever British bird) by law in 1534 under Henry VIII, when the penalty was: *'paine of imprisonment for one yeare, and to lose and forfeit for every egge of any Bustarde so taken or distroid xx pence.'*

THE MALE GREAT BUSTARD is 1 metre tall and turkey-like, with brown and ochre barred back, chestnut breast, black flight feathers and white secondaries in the wing. He has a magnificent display in which he lowers his wings, throws out his chest and turns wings and tail bottom up, making himself into a large off-white ball. Viewing of birds can be arranged through The Great Bustard Group – search online for details.

BARN OWLS HAD been suffering a huge decrease in Britain (and Europe and the USA), but since 1995 the trend here has been reversed and a six-fold increase has been noted. The best way to help them is to put up a nest-box on your farm building or country cottage. Check the RSPB website for details of sale or how to build.

LONG-EARED AND SHORT-EARED Owls have in the past roosted together in winter, using hedgerow bushes on east-coast farmland. Although 50 birds may have been seen together in the past, this no longer occurs and only a few birds are still recorded today.

REED BUNTINGS OFTEN breed these days in rape fields and young forest plantations. The male with black head and chest, white collar and striped chestnut/ black wings, sits atop a flowering plant repeating his simple song rather in the manner of a sparrow. About 300,000 birds are scattered over the farms, forests, and marshes of Britain in summer or winter. They are affected by snow as they are then unable to find grass and weed seeds.

Moor and Mountain

PTARMIGAN MALES NOW become almost pure white in the third and final moult of the year. Their backs retain the palest grey shades until the last. Tail feathers remain black and so does the eye-stripe. A red wattle above the eye cannot be seen unless one is close. The shape of the bird is beautifully adapted to the snowy hummocks and small boulders among the heather so you could almost walk onto it as it crouches on the mountain slope. What a surprise, then, as part of the ground erupts at your feet with a rapid whirr of wings and then glides at terrific speed across the slopes.

THE RAVEN IS found across the whole of the northern hemisphere. Scottish birds find Highland winters quite easy-going with a good supply of dead carcasses such as starved deer, sheep and the leftover morsels from Golden and White-tailed Eagle kills. Ravens will be the first to find dead Grouse and Ptarmigan in the bitter arctic winter.

HOODED CROWS WILL follow behind Ravens and feed second in the carrion chain. They are capable of flying down smaller birds and grappling them to the ground when the marlin spike of their beak quickly beats the victim to death. This grey Crow has a smaller world range outside Britain, being found only in Scandinavia and Russia to the Urals.

SNOWY OWLS HAVE a high northern range from Iceland to Lapland. This includes the Shetlands where they bred in 1967 and 1968. Sporadic sightings of these magnificent birds can occur right across the country during hard winter months. My father knew of a bird that was swept south to the Devonshire coast in the 1920s. He wrote about it in his book *Tarka the Otter*, calling it Bubu the Terrible (Latin name is *Bubu scandiacus*):

> The north wind carried a strange thickset bird which drifted without feather sound. Its plumage was white, barred and spotted with dark brown. Its fierce eyes were ringed with yellow, the colour of the lichen on the stone shippens. Mile after mile its soft and silent wings had carried it, from a frozen land where the Northern Lights stared in stark perpetuity upon the ice-fields. The thick-set bird was an Arctic Owl, and its name was Bubu, which means terrible. It quartered the mires and the burrows, and the gripe of its feathered feet was death to many ducks and rabbits.

Sightings

1
....

2
....

3
....

4
....

5
....

6
....

7
....

8
....

9
....

10
....

11
....

12
....

13
....

14
....

December

15
....

16
....

17
....

18
....

19
....

20
....

21
....

22
....

23
....

24
....

25
....

26
....

27
....

28
....

29
....

30
....

31
....

Index of Bird Names

52
Favourite
West Sussex
Walks

Richard Williamson

52 FAVOURITE WEST SUSSEX WALKS

Richard Williamson

ISBN: 978-1-84953-233-4   Hardback   £9.99

Richard Williamson's weekly walking column has long been one of the most popular features in the *Chichester Observer* and *West Sussex Gazette*. Now, following the format that has proved such a hit over the years, for the first time he has compiled his favourite walks – one for every week of the year – with hand-drawn route maps. His knowledge and love of the timeless South Downs landscape and its varied flora, fauna and stories – from bat-birds and the Devil's Jumps to beloved pubs and famous poets – combine with practical notes on routes that can be covered easily in an afternoon.

'If you fancy a walk… all you need is this great pocket guide… there really is fun for all the family.'

Primary Times

'His friendly, folksy style encourages the walker to revel in the journey and sights to be seen rather than regard it as a set task to be completed before nightfall…

Sussex Life magazine

If you're interested in finding out more about
our books, find us on Facebook at
Summersdale Publishers
and follow us on Twitter at
@summersdale.

www.summersdale.com